Becoming an Employer of Choice

Make your organisation a place where people want to do great work

Judith Leary-Joyce

Judith Leary-Joyce is an expert in leadership and management. She is CEO of Great Companies Consulting (www.greatcompaniesconsulting.com), which she set up in 2002 after spending the previous year working on the Sunday Times 100 Best Companies to Work For list. GCC helps companies build workplaces that make a positive contribution to the life of employees, whilst being successful in the market place. She is a board member of the [...] Leadership Centre for the UK. With a background in Gestalt psychology, she was a founder member and MD of the Gestalt Centre, a Psychotherapy [...] She can be contacted at judith@greatcompaniesconsul[...]

Dedication

To everyone who works in an organisation.

We all deserve Great Companies.
And we are all responsible for creating them.

Until one is committed, there is hesitancy, the chance to draw back, always ineffectiveness. . . .

The moment one definitely commits oneself, then Providence moves, too. . . .

Whatever you can do,
or dream you can,
begin it.
Boldness has genius, power and imagination in it.

Johann Wolfgang von Goethe (1749–1832)

The Chartered Institute of Personnel and Development is the leading publisher of books and reports for personnel and training professionals, students, and all those concerned with the effective management and development of people at work. For details of all our titles, please contact the publishing department:
Tel: 020-8263 3387
Fax: 020-8263 3850
E-mail: publish@cipd.co.uk
The catalogue of all CIPD titles can be viewed on the CIPD website:
www.cipd.co.uk/bookstore

Becoming an Employer of Choice
Make your organisation a place where people want to do great work

Judith Leary-Joyce

Chartered Institute of Personnel and Development

Published by the Chartered Institute of Personnel and Development,
CIPD House, Camp Road, London, SW19 4UX

First published 2004
Reprinted 2004

Designed and typeset by Fakenham Photosetting, Fakenham, Norfolk
Printed in Great Britain by The Cromwell Press, Trowbridge, Wiltshire

British Library Cataloguing in Publication Data
A catalogue of this publication is available from the British Library

ISBN 1 84398 057 6

Chartered Institute of Personnel and Development, CIPD House,
Camp Road, London, SW19 4UX
Tel: 020 8971 9000   Fax: 020 8263 3333
Email: cipd@cipd.co.uk   Website: www.cipd.co.uk
Incorporated by Royal Charter. Registered Charity No. 1079797

Contents

List of tables

Appreciations

This is how it works. You have an outrageous idea about writing a book. You get all excited about who you'll thank – Oscar-style, of course. Then the cold reality hits, and you come down to earth with a tremendous thump!

I am meant to say that I could not have done it alone. In fact, when it got to putting finger to keyboard, I discovered just how totally alone I was. It was up to me – was I going to write this or not? However, without my daughter Miriam and my husband John I would have gone barmy. My daughter Martha became my part-time editor and saved you all from weird spellings, nonsensical apostrophes and those wise ideas that felt great at the time, but didn't work the next day. My dear friend Helen Fatir has also been a constant source of support during the miseries.

I have had such an exciting time researching this book. I have met wonderful people, spent time in fantastic companies, been on adventures and learned a massive amount. All the companies included in this book have been tremendous in their support – I have thoroughly enjoyed meeting you all, and I look forward to more adventures in the future.

Central to it all is Jonathan Austin, who had the dream, the courage and the panache to convince the *Sunday Times* and the DTI what a great idea it was to have a *100 Best Companies to Work For* list in the UK. The year we spent working together taught me so much, not least the importance of great company culture, and our ongoing friendship is something I really value.

My Great Companies consulting team of amazing consultants have held the faith, supported me and done their best to tend my work/life balance – against the odds, it must be said. Tim Melling, Tony Fraser, Roger Evans and Malcolm Frow taught me much about leadership, management and consulting. Stephen Partridge has been a great editor, believing in what I was doing from our first meeting – it is thanks to him that you are reading this book today.

But what caused me to pick up the opportunities that have led me here? Two kids I remember from my childhood – Bassy and Janet –

who had really tough lives in post-war Wolverhampton. They touched my heart and informed my life's mission – I just always wanted to make it easier for them and others who struggle against the odds. Great company culture is the best way I have found yet. Organisations that respect those who work for them and produce profitable outputs – it's a no-brainer!

Foreword

The *Sunday Times 100 Best Companies to Work For* awards provide Britain's most revealing guide to the firms where people go to work with a spring in their step.

For the 2004 list we captured the opinions of 58,000 employees, and the resulting database is the gold standard in mass human resources research. That database holds the secret of a happy working life – one that is rich in challenge and encouragement.

Judith Leary-Joyce has identified the value of the project and used the research to discover precisely how senior managers create environments in which staff can flourish. One of the key factors is trust. It is a credit to the faith of all those chief executives who take part in Best Companies surveys that they allow their staff to express themselves so freely to a third-party research organisation, especially when there are so many competitive pressures.

It is abundantly clear that best companies to work for do not happen by accident. They are created by managers who follow through their decision with a strategy that permeates every part of their organisation. We have much to learn from them. In these pages you will discover some of the secrets of that best practice.

Richard Caseby, Managing Editor, the *Sunday Times*

Chapter 1

The business case

This chapter could consist of just one statement:

> Great companies consistently outperform the FTSE All Share. Over the past five years the best companies would have earned an investor a compounded annual return of 12.1 per cent, compared with a 5.8 per cent decline in the FTSE All Share index as a whole.
>
> Source: Sunday Times 100 Best Companies to Work For list, 2003
> Statistics by Frank Russell Company

How interested would your shareholders be in your corporate culture if they knew that? They would really want you to become an employer of choice because it is good for the bottom line.

It is a universal truth of business that no matter how unique or innovative your products and systems are, it is only a matter of time before someone else is doing it as well or better than you. If you are a market leader, you have to keep running hard to stay ahead of the hounds snapping at your heels, and if you are one of the chasing pack, you will get breathless just keeping up.

The only thing your competitors cannot copy – your only truly unique and lasting competitive edge – is your people. That familiar rhetoric of the annual report is true: your people really are your greatest asset. Or they will be, if you build a work environment in which they can shine.

It is not worth worrying that others might pinch your ideas and products – they definitely will, alongside undercutting your price. Better to utilise your people to the full and go right on leading the field, while they struggle to keep up. But how to do that? This book is full of thoughts and ideas from those named as Great Companies. And the facts below and in the draft presentation in Appendix 3 give you even more reason to read on.

The Facts

In short, great company culture will give you:

- easy recruitment
- powerful retention
- high levels of creativity and innovation
- improved customer service
- a great workplace that customers like too.

Easy recruitment

Once people hear what an exciting workplace you have, they will flock to join you. Those companies that made it into the *Sunday Times 100 Best Companies to Work For* list have proved this in spades. Timpson is a perfect example of this.

In 2001, prior to the publication of the *50 Best Companies to Work For* list, Timpson had 80 per cent employment. After publication this increased to 100 per cent. And by 2002, when named again as one of the *100 Best Companies to Work For*, Timpson had a waiting list and was attracting women and graduates for the first time. The end result is a jump in profits from £3 million in 2001 to £6.5 million in 2003.

Such is the power of great company culture – energetic, dynamic people want to work with you, knowing they will enjoy their work and develop their career into the bargain. The business can choose the best person for the job, providing the very best option for success.

Powerful retention

Once people realise they are in a good workplace, they want to stay. Great companies develop careers in house – growing their own to make sure they keep all the expertise and experience. They also involve colleagues in seeking the best way to run the business, listening to their ideas and concerns from the front line. What young high-potential person can resist that? From the moment they walk through the door, management are paying attention, listening well and looking to three jobs down the line – it is a compelling argument for commitment. Especially when linked to a challenging and honest workplace.

Claridges demonstrate this well. They instigated a major culture change, including consulting colleagues on what changes were necessary in the business, and daily staff briefings. The end result was that staff turnover reduced from 73 per cent to 16 per cent in five years.

Imagine the bottom-line impact when recruitment costs fall and less time is lost as the outgoing person shifts his or her attention away from the work and the incoming arrival strives to grasp the intricacies of a new job.

High levels of creativity and innovation

Provide challenge and support in appropriate balance and you will stimulate the creative juices. Couple this with a strong feeling of belonging so that people speak of the workplace as 'their company' and 'like family' and you have a heady mix for any growing business. Everyone in the organisation takes responsibility and focuses on what will serve the business best. People who feel an attachment to the community watch for pitfalls and have great ideas about how to deal with them.

Hiscox are a prime example. They were part of the syndicate that insured the World Trade Centre, so business took a major hit in 2001. Because their commitment to colleagues includes appreciating the wisdom of experience, they were able to ride the storm and bring the business to a better position within the year.

Improved customer service

The very best customer service operations have excellent people cultures. We can give only as much as we receive. Just like money: if we have it, we can enjoy spending it; when we are broke, we get depressed or borrow – which costs us dear in the long run. It is the same with customer relationships: people cannot give what they do not have, and if they try to give what is not real for them, it will cost everyone dear in the long run.

Take Flight Centre. Strong working relationships encourage colleagues to build equally strong relationships with customers, who then return to them time and again for help. The end result is 23 new shops and businesses opened in 2002, giving a jump in turnover of 36 per cent, leading to a 100 per cent increase in profits.

People who feel cared for, respected and valued give high-quality customer service, building loyal and committed relationships that are more effective than the very best marketing and PR.

Customers like great workplaces

In this day and age, ethics in business has a high profile. People will take their custom away from organisations that do not live up to expected standards, so being known as a great workplace will help differentiate you from competitors. When faced with a choice of provider, people are more likely to go for the company that is known as a fantastic employer. Supporting an organisation that exploits colleagues is not a good option.

TD Industries are known for high trust and integrity by partners (employees), suppliers and customers. To quote Jack Lowe Jnr, the CEO:

> I am convinced that high trust has allowed us to be agile and aggressive during these difficult economic times and continue to outperform our industry. TD always emerges from difficult times with a strengthened position in our marketplace.

To test his judgement on this, look at the graph on slide number 9 in the business case/evidence (Appendix 3) – it speaks volumes.

More facts
Low trust costs you money

People will concentrate on looking after themselves if they do not trust the organisation. This leads to higher costs as they cover their backs and take the safest options on suppliers, etc. When trust is high, people look for the best options, build strong supplier relationships and costs go down.

See the research findings on slide 7 of Appendix 3.

Retention figures drop

Each new recruit costs you twice the annual salary. See your retention figures improve by 10 to 20 per cent and you are making a real saving to the bottom line.

See the figures on slide 5 of Appendix 3, and compare those of your sector.

Recruitment becomes easier

Once yours is known as a great workplace, people want to join and their applications increase. When people love their work, they talk about it and encourage suitable people to apply for a job – so some of the vetting will have been done for you.

See the recruitment results on slide 20 of Appendix 3.

Leadership affects the bottom line

Sound leadership respects people and provides them with the environment in which they can do their best work. Holding the power lightly and sharing responsibility makes the best of talent and impacts directly on the results of the business.

See the results of TD Industries once they instigated Servant Leadership – slide 9 of Appendix 3.

What gets measured gets done

Great companies set clear measures, then reward and celebrate success. People feel valued and see the benefits of doing a great job. Whether rewards are financial or through public appreciation, the results impact on the bottom line.

See the achievements of Flight Centre, slide 13 of Appendix 3.

Two-way communication is a business necessity

Giving information from the top is generally accepted; receiving it from below is often forgotten. Two-way communication ensures buy-in and commitment to the company, which pays off in direct improvement in performance.

See the Claridges results from a culture change, slide 23 of Appendix 3.

Conclusion

It may not be easy, but it is worth it. Great companies benefit in numerous ways – many that cannot be quantified. But the bottom line figures speak for themselves.

Even when you are an employer of choice, there will be difficult times: you will be prone to the same vagaries of the market as every other company. But do expect your people to pull out all the stops to give the company the best possible chance, and to stay loyal through the toughest of times. Care for them well at all times and they will return the favour tenfold.

Chapter 2

How to use this book

Great companies are inspirational places. Because we are not all fortunate enough to work in them, this book is designed to give insight into how they work and the benefits they provide.

You can read the book from front to back or choose the chapters most relevant to your present need. There are specific stories detailing what these companies do, some of which you will be able to try for yourself, plus additional ideas for action.

These companies build high levels of trust because they really care about their people and are consistent in their behaviour. Easy to say, I know – but if they can do it, so can you. Whether you are in the private sector, not-for-profit or public sector, you work with people. People in every work environment will respond to the behaviours and ideas in this book. So don't be put off trying, and don't worry if the idea comes from a different sector.

Do not be put off by your position in the organisation either. Received wisdom is that these changes must always begin at the top, so if the senior leaders are not with you, it will not work. There is a truth in this – it will certainly be a lot easier and quicker if the desire for a great company culture comes from the top down.

However, you can create change from a middle management position. Develop a centre of excellence in your own team. Begin in your sphere of influence and take every opportunity to spread the word. As your team thrives, people will be interested in what you are doing. They will want some of what you have – your sphere of influence will grow and you will be on your way to critical mass.

Wherever the initiative starts, it is not an easy job. There is no magic formula that will transform the workplace overnight. The magic lies in being consistent and actually doing the things others only talk about – over and over again.

Remember: a great company culture is a living entity, needing constant care and attention. At the time of writing, all the companies mentioned are great in the ways described. However, they also know that if they take their eye off the ball, they may fall over. It is a constant effort to keep the culture strong and productive.

You may have heard contrary things about the companies mentioned, but resist the temptation to judge. A company may be great for those who work there, but what suits one will not suit everyone. Be willing to look through the eyes of company colleagues and see what they see. It will be great practice for understanding your own colleagues – understanding what the world looks like for them will teach you a great deal.

Basic assumptions

I have written this book around certain assumptions:

- Everyone has potential and if that potential is unleashed, everyone can achieve extraordinary things. Because organisations are made up of people, they also have the chance of being extraordinary – if they provide the environment in which people can access their potential.
- People seek out employers that provide that environment. Everyone wants to do a great job – to go home at the end of the day and feel satisfied. They want to unleash their potential, to be the best they can be, so they look for the places that will help them do that.
- This fits with present-day expectations of work overall. Few companies offer a job for life any more. People move from job to job, seeking the best career path, accepting that change is a constant. People must be robust, strong and flexible and willing to make the most of every situation.
- The companies that do best in this new work environment make a different pact. They encourage, support and enable colleagues to do their best work, trusting that the company will gain.
- Such companies make no demands about commitment or loyalty; instead, they strive to earn it. They realise that staying in a job because you have to is not a recipe for success, so they provide an environment that is challenging, inspiring and fun, so that people choose to stay.
- Change is a constant, and successful people welcome it. Change is not something to do, it is something we need to allow. Huge

amounts of energy go into resisting change, regardless of its value –
we are creatures of the familiar. Once you stop resisting, change happens all on its own. So the real task of change is to remove the obstacles or barriers that make people wary and risk-averse. All of this
is dependent on trust levels. When trust is high, people can be open
and change is less of a threat.

The paradox of great companies

Great organisations accept the new order, understanding that people
move around more than in the past and that they must vie for the best
talent.

The paradox is that where there is a great company culture, people
choose to stay; which keeps the expertise and knowledge in-house and
builds a highly effective business.

Employer of choice

Being an employer of choice means you have to honour this pact. If you
want the best people to work with you and build your business, you
must:

- provide an environment in which colleagues can thrive and shine
- support and challenge them to access the best in themselves
- set high standards and be rigorous in appraisal
- build strong relationships, understanding the talents, strengths and
  needs of individual people
- acknowledge and celebrate success – make work a joy as well as a job
- build high trust throughout the company – it is the only way to get
  the best from people
- be a model in your own work – stretch yourself, live the company
  principles, have fun, work hard and celebrate your success.

Developing the right attitude

Great cultures need great leaders – not just those who sit at the top of
the organisation, but throughout the company. Cultivate a leadership
approach to life, whatever your job, and you will add value to a great
company.

The cultures that nurture this approach engage in 'servant leadership' – a style of relating common to all the great companies included

in this book. Not all of them call it by that name, but it defines the way people throughout the company behave towards each other.

Essentially it means providing, at every level of the organisation:

- a clear, understandable rationale for the business – an inspiring vision to follow, a sound strategy for action and clear measures so that success is identifiable
- *service*, placing each colleague in an environment that supports their very best work – ie asking 'How can we help you?', 'What do you need?', 'What will help you do a great job?'

This applies both to those with 'leader' in their title and to everyone else. Every manager must help their people understand their work in the context of the business, and every manager must enable – serve – those who follow them, providing an environment in which they can do their best work.

To cultivate this in your workplace, be prepared to:

- listen well – You can serve only when you know what the other person needs. Taking time to listen to concerns and ideas is the most positive way to create a great culture. So practise listening skills and resist the temptation to talk first.
- explore understanding – Make sure everyone you work with understands where they fit into the business. Whether you have one direct report or lead a division of 2,000, each person must recognise the impact their work makes on the success of the whole. Help your people to see the value they add and they will work in quite a different way.
- challenge the status quo – Do not accept behaviours and actions just because it is what you always do and it makes life easier. Be rigorous in expectations of yourself and those you work with. This will bring creativity and excitement to the workplace. Remember: everyone wants to do a good job. If you expect it of them, standards will rise.
- be honest – Great teams/organisations have trust at their heart. Deliver tough and pleasant messages with equal honesty. Make sure people know where they stand and you will earn loyalty in the long term.
- live your guiding principles – Do not leave those principles/values in the desk drawer. Incorporate them into your day-to-day behaviour. Be a role model of a great manager/leader and treat others as you want to be treated yourself.

- keep track of your own impact and gather feedback regularly. It is really easy to get into a rut of behaviour. We all have our little habits and rarely realise how irritating/counterproductive they can be for others. Stay in touch with your impact by inviting feedback, cultivating open relationships where people are not afraid to challenge you, and taking time out for your own development.

Developing your thinking

To help you begin thinking great-company-style, I have used language and an approach that is appropriate to great company culture:

Colleagues

People who work in these companies are rarely referred to as 'employees' or 'staff'. This is about being clear from the outset that everyone is in this together, using all the talent available for the good of the organisation. Seeing everyone as a colleague demonstrates the lack of hierarchy and the inclusion needed to create such a positive culture. I have chosen to use this word throughout to begin that challenge of seeing everyone in this way.

Guiding principles

This is a term I now use as a result of talking with many companies, great and not so great, about their values. All too often these days, values are associated with the brand, by which they describe the way we relate to our business and the image we wish to project in the world. This is not the same as how we behave towards each other on a day-to-day basis. By referring instead to the guiding principles, we can differentiate and clarify the behaviours and beliefs that we choose to follow *on principle*.

Repetition

The great company model is totally 'joined up', so it is inevitable that there will be some repetition in places. Also, to allow for readers who choose to look only at specific areas, I have tried to give as clear a picture as possible in each chapter. So if you notice this happening, take a moment to see how the specific issue relates to that element of the model and how you can use it to best effect. You will then have further knowledge to add to what you read next time you meet it.

Next steps

You may be reading this book to improve what is already a great company or through a longing to develop a better workplace for yourself. There are numerous ideas in this book that you can pinch. Think about your organisation's environment and work out the best way to use an idea. Remember: each great company has its own signature – its own version of greatness. So take the idea and customise it to your organisation.

Do not expect to get it right first time. Get your team on board and work on it together. When an idea fails, take a deep breath, identify what went wrong, and try again. The act of exploration will be just as effective in building trust as the perfect outcome. In fact, it could even be better.

It will always be tempting to put these ideas on the back burner – after all, you are extremely busy, e-mails overwhelm you, the phone never stops ringing, and there are endless meetings to attend – never mind appraisals to do and reports to write. When the pressure is on, it is so easy to slip back and focus only on the immediate task. Contributing to great company culture will take time, but it is actually part of your work as a manager or leader. Ignore it and it will cost you even more time. Accept it, it will pay back huge dividends.

Equally, do not expect other people to join in without a struggle. Everyone is busy, and a plea for change is not always easily received. There will be times when you feel as if you have run directly into a brick wall – so be prepared for it.

Mr Honda understood this: 'I failed in 99 per cent of my attempts in order to succeed in the remaining 1 per cent.' It takes focus, determination and total commitment to keep going in the face of adversity, plus good friends who understand why it matters, who will accept the periodic rant and who will help you refocus and begin again.

Change is never easy, so find support at the outset.

- Take a good look at the book and find ideas that excite you.
- Identify the people most likely to support you. If this is your leader/manager, include them as soon as you can. If not, be prepared to seek out other great managers wherever you can find them.
- Meet up and share your thinking. Have a discussion about the possibilities, building on each other's ideas. Do this in great company manner from the outset – listen well, challenge, celebrate finding each other, have fun.

- Share networks: see who has access to sympathetic senior leaders; find other advocates to join you.
- Set up formal or informal meetings to stay in touch and share learning.
- Keep records of the process – achievements and failures plus the learning that went with both. Be prepared to share these with anyone who is interested.
- Read through the successes when you are feeling down to remind yourself of how far you have come.

In time you will make an impact beyond your immediate sphere of influence. The word will get round and other people will want what you have. The rumour mill is a great thing at times like these. Building a centre of excellence in your team will encourage others to find out what you do and follow suit.

It can be a slow business, but the moment you actively choose to be a great manager, your workplace will change for the better.

Another way to understand this process is outlined by John Crabtree, Senior Partner at Wragge & Co.

The ham sandwich principle

'Cast your bread upon the water and it will come back a ham sandwich'
I asked John what his leadership philosophy was, and this is what he told me. It took me a moment to understand – my mind filled up with images of soggy bread sinking in a murky river – but then I recognised the sentiment. It is a philosophy put forward by all the significant spiritual disciplines: give freely, and you will receive in return.

The way John explained it is 'Go about your business in a helpful and supportive way, pushing yourself out, giving bits of yourself everywhere – putting the bread on the water. It'll all come back. You won't just get the bread back – it will come back with butter on it, and if you're very good, it'll come back as a ham sandwich. It just makes you smile, that you do something just because you think you should or it would be nice to do it, and in some totally unconnected way, a year later, a major universal, intergalactic, corporate holdings plc calls and says, "We gather you did something a year ago at such-and-such, and we want to give you some work." If you have that approach to your work, it always comes back in some experience.'

John had grown up with the saying 'Cast your bread upon the water and it comes back buttered.' It was the day he visited an art gallery in Dartmouth that extended his reach to sandwiches. Walking in the door the first thing he saw was a fantastic painting of a ham sandwich bouncing off the water! While looking at the painting, John got into conversation with the artist. Now the artist was fond of the picture, having painted it in memory of his grandfather, and it was not for sale. 'I told him about my saying, and he said, "Here you are – you can have it for 50 quid." So I bought it from him.'

'So many bits about Wragge & Co. are ham sandwiches – I don't say it any more, because they get fed up with my jargon. Partners are doing things because they think it's what they should do. Sometimes they recognise things come back because of their actions. Once you have that cause-and-effect it is very powerful.'

Driving home, pondering on our conversation, I realised that this is what great companies do all the time. They are generous in offering support to colleagues and suppliers, knowing that giving will have wider implications. When colleagues see interest and concern from their employer, they want to do the best they can – you'll be familiar with this by the time you reach the end of this book. Like the Asda colleague who was offered an unexpected promotion in a brand new area. It was a major challenge, and one he would have been tempted to refuse if his boss had not been so positive and sure he could do it. With plenty of encouragement and the support to match, he made a stunning job of it. He produced a ham sandwich!

The truly great companies have strong values and work to those every day – 'because it's the right thing to do'. And as Goethe said, 'Once you truly commit, providence moves.' All manner of unexpected things happen in response, once those principles are acted out for real and not just hung on the wall of the office.

Action steps

- How often do you 'cast your bread upon the water' just for the sake of it – give generously of yourself because it is the right thing to do?

- Can you think of times when the ham sandwich has returned to you – when people have responded to your generosity with an equal and opposite force?
- Think about the day ahead of you – choose one action that is important and matters, but is not urgent, and put it at the top of the list. Do this each day and notice where the ham sandwich comes from.

Chapter 3

Mean what you say: making your reality match your principles

'Treat a colleague badly, and within two weeks they will treat a customer badly.' Tony DeNunzio, CEO of Asda, understands the business significance of making principles live. Leave the good intention to care for colleagues mouldering in your desk drawer and you are storing up a poor customer service record. Bring it into everyday life, and loyalty, service and commitment begin to shine through.

At Asda, leaders see their job as serving colleagues, ensuring that they receive the same level of care as customers. For example, they work to the 'sundown rule': any issues that come to Asda House from the stores are sorted by the end of the day – and there is a 'sundown sheriff' to measure and ensure that this is happening. No waiting weeks or even months to hear back from those magical people at the top of the tree who are too busy to take the time on a 'minor' problem.

Imagine how this impacts on managers and colleagues working at the sharp end with supplier problems or tricky customers, striving to do their best job. Knowing the leaders at head office are available when they need them makes a major difference. They are definitely not alone, it is a team effort at Asda – but they are not unusual. This theme is common in great companies: they do what they say they will do, and are measured on it to ensure that it is not just rhetoric.

I can hear the cry already: 'I just don't have time to do that. It's easier for them.'

This is where principles come in – by helping you decide priorities. I do not for a moment suggest this is easy – in fact, I know it definitely is not. But that does not mean it is not the right thing to do.

Despite all the rationalisations that will come to mind, consider the following questions:

- Think of a specific time when you had a request for action/advice that you put to one side.
- What was the impact of your non-action? Did you hold up the work? How much time was spent in trying to get hold of your answer?
- What was the impact on the customer sitting at the end of the chain?

I suspect you had a profound effect on a number of people. The 'sundown rule' builds trust, raises standards throughout the company and provides excellent service for the customer. If you want this in your company:

- Go through the issues on your desk, including requests for action.
- Using the time management 'Important' and 'Urgent' boxes (see Table 1), allocate each issue to one box. Be mindful of your principles as you do this. You will be tempted to put most things in the Important/Urgent box – do not give in to that temptation. Restrict yourself to a maximum of 25 per cent!
- This will form the basis of your actions today. Your first action will be to inform those low on the priority list that you will not respond quickly, to suggest a better person to speak to, or to say when you will get back to them.
- You will have to deal with those that are Urgent and Important at this point. In the longer term, your aim is to work from the Important/Not Urgent box. This provides maximum support for those who await your outputs and takes much of the stress out of the working day, thereby ensuring that you can do your best work.
- If you have so much that you cannot work your way out of the Important/Urgent box – speak to your manager about support and/or look to what you can delegate.

	Urgent	Not urgent
TABLE 1 **TIME MANAGEMENT: IMPORTANT/URGENT TASKS**		
Important	You will want to put everything into this box. Restrict yourself to 25% and work at reducing it further. Some emergencies will always crop up.	This is where you are aiming to work in the long term. If you are effective, the number of urgent issues will be significantly reduced.
Not important	If something is not important to the business, why are you doing it? Consider if it needs doing at all, and if it does, whether you are the right person to be doing it.	Watch out for these tasks. Although they are easy to do and to cross off your list, they take time and have little impact on the business.

Many companies have principles about being respectful of people, chosen and acted on with great effort and care. The facility to speak to senior leaders is one way of honouring this and it makes good business sense. Keeping everyone in the loop, top down and bottom up, ensures that nothing gets lost.

Some companies have 'skip-level meetings', in which senior leaders meet colleagues from two to three layers down to find out what life is like in their part of the business. This can be done over lunch or a coffee, in general discussion or a question-and-answer session. Others spend time going back to the floor regularly, on the basis that working alongside someone makes conversation easier. E-mail is another way to reach the senior leaders with ideas, as long as the leaders involved are good at handling their e-mail.

Any idea is only as effective as those taking part. To listen and not act will always cost in terms of trust. I recall well the disillusionment of one woman who sent a suggestion to the CEO by e-mail. After six months she re-sent it, only to be ignored again. How does that feel? These leaders say they want to hear from people, but their behaviour belies the fine words. Those moments are defining of future attachment

– every let-down costs a little more heart, until the person leaves or settles for doing a 'good enough' job, saving their excitement and enthusiasm for elsewhere in their lives – and this has a direct impact on the bottom line.

The importance of congruence

Overt behaviour determines the actual guiding principles of a business community. Remember that alarming statistic we hear in presentation skills training – only 7 per cent of what people take in is from what you say, the rest comes from body language, voice tone and behaviour. This is how principles are born – through the day-to-day behaviour of the significant leaders and influencers.

Great companies ensure that behaviour matches words. They strive constantly to be congruent with their principles. This is a major thrust of the great company concept – be congruent. At St Luke's when people working on the Hub – their term for 'reception' – spoke to Neil, the MD, about a lack of respect from some colleagues, the word was sent out through the community. As everyone become more aware, the behaviour changed. In most companies this would have been ignored, or worse, never known, until the receptionist left, allowing the behaviour to persist. Addressing it directly strengthens the culture – every time good intentions are followed through in behaviour, the message gets stronger.

However, there are many financially successful companies that do not have great company cultures, even though they behave in ways that are congruent with their principles. Success lies in congruence; the added factor of greatness lies in the intention behind the principles themselves.

The production of a healthy bottom line is key to the value set of those who define success as profit. They also recognise that people are vital to the process – after all, a company is only a collection of people – so this will be included in the list of principles. So far so good.

The intention that underpins the culture of the company often shows only in the balance and order of the specific principles, making clear where the priorities lie. Financially successful companies put healthy profit/bottom line at the top of the list; great companies make people the headline.

The basic assumptions that underpin this ordering are fundamental to the concept of great company culture. Where money is the priority, the individual is more highly prized; where people are the priority, the success of the company is highly prized by everyone, bringing greater power to bear on the job at hand. But it does require the guts to go against the norms of our present society. See Table 2.

TABLE 2
CONGRUENCE AND CULTURE: DIFFERENCES BY PEOPLE FIT AND PRINCIPLES

	'ME' PRINCIPLES	'ME + YOU' PRINCIPLES
Right people fit	*Successful company*	*Great Company*
	Good financial results	Good financial results
	Stock market happy	Stock market happy
	People valued for what they bring	People valued for who they are
	Commitment depends on career prospects	Commitment is to well-being of company
	Good customer service for business reasons	Excellent customer service from the heart
	Recruitment at any level of the company	Recruitment mostly at entry level
	Belonging limited to personal friendships in company	Strong sense of belonging – 'this is my family'
	Career development based on needs of CV	Career development in-house
	Look after self in tough times	Look after each other in tough times
	Personal development may be risky	Personal development valued
Poor people fit	*Employer of last resort*	*Improving company*
	Feedback/appraisal is low priority and indirect	Feedback/appraisal is high priority and honest
	Poor work may be tolerated, to avoid giving honest feedback	Poor work is identified and addressed immediately
	Person left in the same job or put into a backwater	Right job is sought for the person, to ensure that they can give of their best
	If the right job does not exist, the person is left where they are	If the right job does not exist, the person is asked to leave
	Business changes are used as an opportunity to remove poor performers	Any leavers are dealt with as well as possible, out of respect

Why do we work?

The central question is: why do we go to work in the first place? Money is a key driver, answering the need for home, warmth, food, and safety. We have all experienced feeling insecure in some way or other – some unfortunately with a greater degree of urgency than others. Facing the loss of job and money raises fear and panic; it touches the raw nerve that ensures survival of the race. This alone is enough to take most of us to work each day.

However, once that basic need is answered, other elements kick in. There is little worse than a boring job or a bully boss. Once we know we can eat, it is natural to look for human warmth from those around you – and let's face it, we spend a good portion of our lives at work, so a sterile or hostile environment is not conducive to a good life.

John and James Timpson know the importance of providing a good income for their staff, so they have built a business culture where each colleague can earn more through their own endeavours. Yet they also realise the importance of respect and fun in the workplace. To take account of this they expect all managers to know their staff well – and they model it themselves. They further ensure times of fun and celebration by funding a hearty bar bill at regular intervals – the source of a great time in the Timpson culture. The payback is worth its weight in gold, never mind pints – people are totally committed to the company and strive to do their best work.

There is a third desire in human beings and that is to achieve our best. How 'best' is defined will determine whether work plays a part in achieving this fundamental urge. Maslow called it the drive for self-actualisation. The rest of us talk about the sense of achievement and satisfaction when we surpass expectations and experience the strengthening of self-esteem that goes with success. Put this into the equation and work takes on a different hue.

Take my writing this book. The dream of writing sat idly in the back of my mind for a long time. Then came a discussion with Emma, a young manager in a large blue-chip company, charged with the task of creating a great place to work. In our conversation it became clear there was little information to help her know where to start, and we agreed a first-stage road map was the missing link. I did not know how or what, but I did know I had at least to try.

There followed two years of brewing, researching, and learning about publishers and what would give most benefit to the reader. Then came the task of focusing on the words themselves. I have learned so much about single-mindedness, determination, commitment; I have also made new friends, stretched my thinking, been delighted and utterly frustrated all at once. As the end draws near, I have done more than I ever thought I could do, and have developed as a result. And hopefully you will do the same – by my stretching, I can help you stretch, which will help others to stretch. This is what self-actualisation is about – discovering our own potential and enabling others in the process.

Work as a self-fulfilling prophecy

These different drivers determine how much we put into work, and the effectiveness of a company culture is determined by how high the company aims, both for its own sake and for the sake of the people.

In the distant past of management theories, McGregor spoke of Theory X, a management style built on the assumption that no one wants to work for the sake of it. The only reason for working is because you have to earn enough money to provide safety and social acceptance. Belief in this demands a particular style of management. People must be given rules and directions to follow: they should not be trusted to do the right thing unless watched over – they will give only what they are told to give, and the 'extra mile' is a matter of compulsion. Essentially, they will do a job for the sake of the money alone without commitment or loyalty to the company.

This description may sound extreme and outdated, but there are companies and managers who still hold this view, although probably not entirely consciously. It will be held in the principles of 'put the company first', punitive reactions to mistakes, redundancy as first call when the market shows signs of strain, horror stories of sacking by text message.

Low-trust cultures are based on the assumption that people will look out only for number one. Of course, the irony is that they also create the behaviour they are concerned about – it is a process of wish-fulfilment. If a company assumes you are not to be trusted, you either look after yourself regardless or you leave. The end result is the culture the leaders expect. The real pity is that low-trust cultures create high costs. Research done by an American national construction research organisation, the Construction Industry Institute, shows that projects in which there is a low level of trust incurred expenses that could have been avoided. The knock-on impact of time to check up on people, greater levels of hierarchy and prolonged decision-making added a significant amount to the bottom line. (See slide 7 in the 'Business case/evidence' presentation, Appendix 3.)

As a comparison, consider what McGregor called Theory Y management, later converted by Maslow to a more rounded Theory Z and recently put into practice by Ricardo Semler at Semco and outlined in his book *The Seven-Day Weekend*. Both are based on the assumption that work is as natural a part of life as rest and play; that people will seek responsibility when they feel committed and involved; and that commitment comes not from fear but from reward, especially the intangible rewards of appreciation and achievement. Maslow added to this the recognition that people want to be creative, proud of what they do, and to make a difference. He would have made a great company leader!

Put that into the work setting and the job of management is quite different. Colleagues need guidelines, not rules. They benefit from encouragement, development and celebration of achievement. Above all they need an environment in which they can explore their potential. The business that provides this level of interest and stimulation is rewarded with high levels of commitment and the benefit of all that creativity and enthusiasm. And, when lined up with the appropriate business strategy, this brings a direct benefit to the bottom line.

The Construction Industry Institute research demonstrates this with hard fact – high-trust cultures in project teams brought a reduction of direct costs. When people are trusted to do the best for the business, there is less need for surveillance and monitoring, and colleagues keep a close eye on expense because they feel part of the company and want to do the most effective job they can.

The intention of principles

How does this relate to great company culture/behaviours being congruent with principles? The difference between 'financially successful' and 'great' lies in the intention behind the guiding principles. Does the company exist purely to make money at whatever cost, or to do so in a way that enables people to fulfil their potential? Paradoxically, the latter makes better financial sense – colleagues working at full stretch in the creative sense will make more impact on the bottom line than those who are just doing the job. It enables the business to run smoothly, with low expense ratios and high levels of commitment.

Essentially it depends whether organisational principles are exclusive or inclusive:

- exclusive organisational principles – The principles are 'self-centred' in a business sense. They take a narrow focus, concentrating only on business outcomes, regardless of the cost to colleagues – ie the principles relate primarily to profits and exclude the needs of others. They also encourage colleagues to behave in a self-centred manner, looking after number one.
- inclusive organisational principles – The principles include everyone. They reflect the business in its widest sense, highlighting the needs and development of colleagues as a strong business driver – ie the principles place as much importance on colleagues as on profits. They encourage behaviour that respects and supports colleagues, customers and the community.

People too can become exclusive in their thinking, especially when working for a company that expresses exclusive principles. They look after their immediate needs, failing to see that work is part of their development. Career promotion becomes an entirely personal task and is generally taken to mean moving companies at regular intervals to ensure a wide range of experience. Commitment to the company is rarely a factor; commitment to personal and financial development is high. Managers will hear of forthcoming moves only when the next advancement is secured and the chance to stop expertise and company knowledge walking out of the door is limited to financial sweeteners. Energy is funnelled into personal development alone, rather than personal and company development as a combined force. We have all heard those discussions – 'It's time I moved on and extended my experience for the sake of my CV.'

This emphasis brings all sorts of knock-on effects. When a manager is not committed to the development of a colleague, confronting poor performance or counter-cultural behaviour is less important. Dealing with these issues can be a great tool for self-development, but in exclusive organisations all too often it is left to fate. The manager hopes someone else will give the necessary feedback, puts the person into a backwater job in the hope it will prompt them to leave, or expects the team to try harder and work round the problem.

In an inclusive company where people are high priority, poor performance will not be tolerated – the under-performing colleague is too important. Tough love comes high on the agenda when principles relate to work as an important part of life.

At Flight Centre they recognise that the company is totally dependent on the effectiveness of its people. They also realise that the longer people stay and the more involved they are in the progress of the business, the better they will serve each other and their customers. They want people to feel excited and fulfilled by their work, while being cared for and encouraged by the company – otherwise, why would they stay? So they have developed 'Brightness of Future' – a theme that runs throughout the company – ensuring that each person is supported to create the life they want, even if that ultimately means leaving Flight Centre. The outcome is a highly successful business, growing 20 per cent year on year globally, even in the tough markets of 2002/2003, staffed by people who grow and develop their skills internally.

Get the right person in the right job

Ensuring that a colleague fits the culture is only the first part of the equation. The next stage is to find the job that suits them best. People do their best work when accessing their natural talents – then they will excel and thrive. Finding the right job is not always easy, and it can take a few attempts before the best place is found.

To make sure this happens, managers track progress closely, watching for signs of talent being left to moulder. Inclusive principles come into their own at this point, using 'problems' as a pointer to understand needs and focus development. When principles are exclusive, it is easier to turn a blind eye and hope for the best.

So regular contact between colleague and manager becomes highly significant. At Asda appraisals are monthly, as they are at Flight Centre – any less frequently and issues/congratulations could go untended. Difficulties are spotted early on and tackled from the perspective of both colleague and manager – ie, is the colleague struggling because they feel unsupported by the boss or is it a matter of expertise or the wrong job? Both parties explore the issues and take part in the solution.

Compare this to an exclusive company where a colleague is not performing. Appraisal is twice-yearly at best, with little contact in between. Everyone knows there is a problem, but they are waiting for the manager to tackle it. She dislikes giving feedback and finds development conversations difficult, so keeps the appraisal short – or even cancels, because 'something has come up'. People in the team gradually pick up the shortfall and the situation is sorted – for a while. Inevitably, resentment builds – why should others do more than their fair share? Why should the individual get away with it? Credibility of the manager drops as time goes by. The end result? High-potential people in the team get fed up and look for other jobs, while the poor performer continues oblivious to their impact on what was a good team. Sound familiar?

Taking the line of least resistance is not an option when inclusive principles are lived from day to day in an organisation. Addressing problems and underperformance is high priority because it impacts on both people and business. If someone fails to pull their weight in a team, it may be they are trying to pull the wrong load. Or it may be that they don't have the support/knowledge they need, or they are having difficulties at home. Whatever the issue, it is for colleague and manager to address together, seeking out the best solution.

Of course, the right job is not always available and there are situations that require tough action to be taken. When exiting is the only way forward, strong people-centred principles demand that it is addressed in a way that serves the business and leaves the person with as much self-esteem as possible. This is part of the paradox. The assumption is that great companies are soft and fluffy, spending time just being nice to people. In fact, they are direct and straightforward, facing up to difficult issues that exclusive companies fight shy of. If you want an easy life, do not go to a great company!

The delight is that when people are significant in the equation and helped to do their very best job, there is huge benefit to the bottom line. Those who function on exclusive principles would hate to think so, but their behaviour costs them profits, as well as high performance and self-esteem.

And where would most of us like to work? In a company that values our contribution, develops potential and promotes as soon as the opportunity arises, keeps us challenged through exciting work and straight feedback, while making every effort to celebrate successes? Or in an organisation that punishes when results are poor; refuses to give straight feedback and so covertly supports poor performance; makes no effort to celebrate success; demonstrates little appreciation unless we are working extra long hours regardless of need, and has precious little fun?

It's a no-brainer. The war for talent has been won by those who live inclusive principles day in, day out.

Summary

- Principles must be clearly understood and agreed by everyone. This process begins as soon as someone starts work, and is reinforced every day.
- When behaviour is consistently in line with principles, people trust more and respect each other. This, in turn, creates trust in the customer.
- We all want to do a good job – it is basic to our sense of self. When people are truly valued and respected, they will do their very best.
- A company can be successful when actions and behaviour are congruent with principles. Only when those principles are people-centred can the company become great.
- Appraisal is an important tool, ensuring that people can use their talents effectively in the right job. Used regularly, it is a positive tool for self and company development.
- Ignoring poor performance is a matter of principle. It demonstrates a lack of respect for colleagues and is a major cost to the business. Great companies 'bite the bullet' and address the issue, seeking the right job for each person.

Respect others – keep track of development

'Respect for others' is a strong principle for Asda, as it is for many other great companies. It is played out on a daily basis in the relationship between colleague and manager. Regular conversation and support ensure that talent is leveraged for the benefit of the business and person alike.

Gal Shivti used to be part of the Retail-tainment team at Asda. He was the one who ensured that we all had a great time doing the shopping, returning later to the car park for a pop concert or a karaoke competition. 'Asda Goes to Trolleywood' was his favourite headline!

But talent is never left to languish at Asda and he was approached by the chief operating officer to see if he would be interested in moving into Dairy to head up the team of buyers. You have to admit that that is a big jump and yoghurt is not necessarily a match for karaoke. He knew little or nothing about the ins and outs of the chill cabinet, but, as Gal says, 'If the company has faith in you, you can believe in yourself.' Knowing that he would be given the support he needed, he took the job on and is having a great time with his new team.

Teamwork is the essence of success for Gal. His team are full of enthusiasm and love for their work and Asda. He puts a huge amount of effort into supporting and challenging them. Everyone writes their own appraisal and, with his input, this forms the basis of their development plan for the year. Their upward appraisal contributes to his own plan. For many companies this is where it ends until appraisal time next year. Such is his commitment to his team of six that Gal sits down each week with everyone to chat through their personal development plan (PDP) for at least an hour. This does not have to be a formal meeting – travelling to a store or taking lunch together is a great opportunity – but one way or another he has that conversation.

Gal is not alone in this level of care. Everyone in Asda has an appraisal meeting each month. Gary Hogan, MD at Flight Centre, agrees strongly that this is the only way to do it. He feels really sorry for the manager who does a yearly appraisal on a colleague's 'day from hell' – it colours the whole year. Yet talk with them regularly about how they are doing and the process becomes highly productive. The concept of underperformance is anathema in great companies – through regular conversation and tracking of the PDP, they 'strike while the iron is hot', before behaviours become embedded and tough to address. Looking for development opportunities, they see the value of acting fast. Plus the fact that if you believe in respecting people, leaving them in the dark is not the right thing to do – for them or for their team.

Action steps

Working closely with your team takes time. If your workload is too heavy to allow this, brush up on the main points of delegation or speak to HR about a course. With the time this frees up:

- Meet with each of your direct reports to find out how they are doing against their personal development plan and agreed objectives.
- Where possible, delegate work that will help them develop skills and talents in an appropriate way.

- If you struggle with appraisals, ask for help from your boss or HR representative to understand more about the process.
- Make sure you understand the talents of each person and be on the lookout for opportunities to develop them.
- If there is an issue that you have been avoiding, look at it from the perspective of the person concerned – what do they need in order to improve performance/do the best job? If you are not clear, ask them directly. Begin by expressing your concern and desire to help. Follow through on agreed actions and allocate time for regular meetings to track progress.
- If someone is underperforming, do not assume that you have to do all the talking. Ask the person how they think they are doing. We generally know when we are not doing well, and it can be a relief to talk about it. Listen to what they have to say, tell the truth, and look for the next steps together.
- Book a time for an appraisal/development discussion with your own boss. Plan which aspect of your work you want to talk about and gather relevant feedback from your direct reports. Afterwards, write out a clear development plan and keep track through regular meetings.

Guiding principles – a yardstick for behaviour

The only way to ensure congruence with principles is to use them as a yardstick of how to behave. Just as vision shows us the direction, principles show us how to get there. But that means that they must be heartfelt, that everyone is comfortable following them – and more important – is not comfortable when they are ignored.

Bob Henry, CEO of CORGI, lives the principles of the company every moment of every day, and in so doing has earned the respect of those who work with him, inside and outside the company.

Principles for him are the yardstick of behaviour, and every business decision is measured against them. When Bob came to CORGI, there was much tightening up to be done both in the way the company worked and in the registration of gas installers. Not a job to be messed with if we are all to sleep safely in our beds at night. If any installers let their training slip, they still retained their registration on the understanding that they would update the training as soon as possible – but that was not always followed up. Changing this meant taking a tough stance that could deprive a gas installer of their ability to work. Clearly a move you and I, as customers, would applaud.

Many of the businesses that register with CORGI thought Bob and his team would not do it. After all, the bottom line would be directly impacted as the income from registration fees were reduced – they thought it was just bluster. In truth, it is a tough decision for any businessperson – to take an action that will cut the bottom line income. What did they do? They made an assessment against their principle – demonstrate commitment. It reads: 'We believe in the fundamental importance of safety and take pride in everything we do. We are committed to a safer world and ensure we always demonstrate professionalism, openness and integrity.'

Really pay attention to a statement like that and the decision is a no-brainer. How could CORGI allow a gas installer to pass the sell-by date of his or her training, when they have a commitment to a safer world and to their integrity? It just could not be done. So the step was taken and the numbers of businesses on the register reduced by about 12 per cent, which directly impacted on CORGI's income and the bottom line. But only for a while – now people know that they cannot afford to let their training go, and the world is a safer place for it.

Action steps

- Check out your company principles. How important are they to you? Under what circumstances would you override them? Use real-time situations to test yourself on the significance. For example, if being really honest with your boss could put your job at risk, what would you do? If a customer was treating one of your people disrespectfully, would you refuse to take the customer's money?
- Take the two most important principles and measure your work and work style against them. Identify how you can be more congruent – ie how you might ensure that your behaviour matches your words.
- The next time you take a decision, consider it from a principles perspective first.
- At the end of your next day at work, review your behaviour. Make a note of those actions that are not in line with principles, and

identify what you should do differently on the next day. Do this on a regular basis. Build it into your day in a positive way, to make sure you do it regularly – for example, use your journey home to look back over the day and assess your effectiveness.

- If you lead a team, talk about the principles and how they fit your work. Ask each person to talk about what they mean to them, and why they are important. Encourage everyone to live according to the principles and give each other feedback on effectiveness.
- Include principles in appraisal/one-to-one discussions.

'Brightness of Future' – building potential

Great companies build the principle of developing people into every moment of the working day. Ensuring that colleagues are stretched and appropriately challenged by their work is one way of building business potential. There is a risk that those you develop move on. A much greater risk is that those you do not develop, stay.

'Our people need to see a clear pathway to achieving their hopes, aspirations and dreams. Flight Centre Ltd is the vehicle for that journey.' This 'Brightness of Future', which drives people forward to discover the best in themselves, depends on leaders who keep a constant eye on their teams' aspirations.

Sonal is a perfect example. She arrived in Flight Centre bearing a degree in fashion plus experience of designing and selling knitwear in New York. Knowing she had not yet found her niche, she spotted an advert for an open interview for FC and decided to attend. It was really tempting – high bonus levels, opportunities for travel, and it sounded like a lot of fun into the bargain, so she decided to give it a go.

Clearly a young woman of energy and enthusiasm, she already has an eye to her future. I met her when she had been with the company for nine months. Describing herself as having been an enthusiastic drifter with little focus, she is now clear she has found the direction she wants. Working at FC she has built confidence in herself and truly believes she can do her best. The job of area leader is already in her sights, and she has put herself down for a training course to flag up her interest. The role is a couple of jumps away, but Brightness of Future means she has a clear development plan, assessed at regular intervals with her team leader to ensure that she has the best chance possible. I was left with no doubt that she will get there at the right time, with the full support of Jo, her own area leader.

Succession planning is not just for the top team. The job of every leader at FC is to ensure that each person, team and area of the business has Brightness of Future. This extends to when people want to leave. Should Sonal decide to go travelling, she and her leader will produce a plan for how she can make enough money to have a really great time. This also diminishes the chance of her clockwatching and reminding her colleagues that she will soon be on Bondi Beach while they are sitting in an office in New Malden. And the chances are that when she returns or wants to work in another country, she'll look to FC for a job.

Action steps

Personally:

- Book a meeting with your boss and ask for feedback on your performance. If you have any concerns about the standard of your work, speak about it and find out how you can improve.
- Talk about your ambitions for the future and find out what you need to do to be ready for an appropriate opportunity.
- If you cannot do this with your own boss, talk with your HR representative and get his or her support for your plans.
- Make sure you have a clear personal development plan, and make notes of your progress.

As a manager:

- Have a conversation with each of your direct reports about their aspirations and hopes for the future. Work out a plan together for how to achieve it, and support them in gaining the necessary experience.
- Be on the lookout for opportunities for people to move on in the business.
- If you see blocks to progress, be clear about this and identify how they can be overcome. If you believe the person has reached their limit, be honest and look for other ways of making the job interesting. Do not allow someone to go forward in hope, if it is not realistic.

Remember: having good people around will reflect well on you, so always know what potential you have in your team. Great managers hire people who are better than themselves.

High-trust cultures and their impact on cost

Where colleagues are trusted and encouraged to make the best of their jobs, they take ownership of the company. From then on, no one will tolerate behaviour that is not good for business, resulting in higher productivity and a reduction in cost.

'Building trusting relationships' and 'responsible behaviour' are guiding principles for TD Industries of Dallas, Texas. Not much new there, I hear you cry – many companies have such fine words in their value set. So let's look at what they actually mean by that. 'We believe people react positively when trust and confidence are placed in them and when the best is expected of them. We try to reflect this belief in all our relationships.' Having visited TD I know this is exactly how they work, even to the point of each person having shares in the company.

Building relationships translates into high expectations of each other. 'We expect people to act responsibly and to work for group goals. We expect them to be dependable and to work hard.' Customers are the direct recipients of that standard, and the company has a reputation for being highly trustworthy.

Combine trust and responsibility and you have a workforce that will reach its full potential, seeking out ways to bring improvement to the end product. Peter worked on the production line and could see the job would be easier and quicker if the sequence was changed. He drew up plans and approached his manager, who agreed it made sense. The change required the line be closed for a day, so they went together to talk to Jack. He was very happy to trust Peter's judgement without needing a major presentation or business case – he just knew Peter cared enough about the company to measure his suggestions against the needs of the customer.

The process was to be rearranged over the weekend, so it was all hands on deck. By the end of the day they were exhausted, but happy with the results. A few beers washed the dust away and it was mission accomplished. The proof was of course in the using – on Monday the line started up and work commenced apace. Productivity increased as everyone did their work in shorter time, just as effectively. From Jack's point of view, trusting Peter made absolute sense – only those doing the work day to day had the expertise to make such decisions. Trusting his colleagues proved better all round – affirmation of Peter, leaner costs, higher productivity and deadlines met in short order.

Action steps

- Think about those you work with – how well do you trust them? Unless they have given you reason not to, consider increasing the trust you give them.
- Identify one area where you could give more responsibility than you do at present. Talk it through with the appropriate person, reassure them that you will give support when needed, set a deadline to check on progress, then leave them to get on with the task.
- If you do not yet have a trusting relationship with your own boss, have a conversation to find out what you can do to improve it.
- Keep everyone in the loop with any changes – make sure that no one feels left out in the cold, not knowing what is happening. This may feel like overkill to begin with, but as trust builds, you can assess the level of communication that will be needed in order to go forward.
- Give direct and honest feedback at all times – make sure that everyone knows where they stand.
- Celebrate successes – even if only with a cuppa and a bun!

Chapter 4

Leadership

Imagine the scene – you spot the CEO's chauffeur-driven car pull into his parking place. You know he will enter the building via his private staircase, sit down in his hushed, elegant office to a cup of coffee out of a silver pot and get news of the day from his equally elegant PA. You know, because you visited him once. The welcome was good, the view fantastic, and the conversation about the new work challenge interesting, but you've never been back.

Rewind. You spot the CEO trying to find a place in the car park. Two days a week he takes his kid to school and so arrives late – always a mistake, parking-wise. He lands in the office and winds his way slowly to his desk against the far wall, chatting to people as he goes – checking up on last night's football with Peter, asking Susan how the parents' evening went, looking at a work problem with Jim. Finally, he sits down at his desk to plan the day. People pass by for a quick word – a problem or a good idea – which he fits in alongside the e-mail and phone messages before going to his first meeting.

Which would you prefer? The more traditional CEO of the 'company royalty' type or the Great Company CEO who is part of the team? Clearly, much will depend on your own view of life and the way you are used to seeing authority. Habit expects the former; personal preference looks for the latter. Research shows the latter to be the more effective in terms of bottom-line figures – so not only is it good from a human perspective, it makes money.

There is something very different about these leaders, which can be summed up in one word: relationships. They are seen around the place – a far cry from the 'royalty' CEO. They know their colleagues and care about them; they inspire, challenge, coach, and have fun. And most important of all, their behaviour matches their words. As a result, they build trust and loyalty – the basis of a great workplace.

Everyone is a leader

Those with senior leadership positions must be able to see the bigger picture and develop appropriate vision and strategy that suits the overall business environment. But they cannot take this vision forward alone. Managers must also be ready to step up to leadership, interpreting the vision for their own area, spotting opportunities as they present themselves, and inspiring those they work with.

'Leaderful' organisations understand that the opportunity for leadership can be picked up by anyone with the drive and enthusiasm to see it through. Creating the environment where people can use their initiative and make the most of their ideas is part of what makes for a great culture.

So as you read this, do not designate it as just for 'them'. The leader at any one moment is just as likely to be you. Pay attention and cultivate leadership behaviour, and you will be ready when the chance presents itself.

What makes a leader?

It begins with the desire to lead. Leadership is both a drive and a calling. We talk a great deal about what leaders do, but far less about the drivers that cause them to take on the task. For some, leadership is an appointed role, sought as the pinnacle of a good career, providing personal challenge, excitement, status and money. It is a formula that underpins many financially sound companies.

For others it is the task that matters and they are willing to put themselves forward, believing they have something to offer. Do not mistake me: this is not entirely altruistic – any leadership task will lead to personal challenge, excitement, and sometimes status and money, but that in itself is not enough. The work must be worthwhile and have a strong purpose. Followers are a high priority, so a healthy, interesting environment is crucial: no one yet built a dynamic and thriving business or project on their own.

Great company leaders come into the latter category. Driven by the personal and business challenge, they also need to achieve something of value. To do this they take their place in the team, serving those who follow, in order that the work is completed effectively. Isolation and deference will not work, nor would they want it.

Take Mick Kent, CEO of Bromford Housing Group. An ambitious man, he became CEO at the age of 31. He describes himself as 'young, naive, pretty incompetent and starry-eyed'. He was running an organisation with 29 people that owned just over 1,000 homes. Now it has 520 people, over 14,000 homes and was named as the fifth best company to work for in the UK in 2003. What was it that drove him to stay there for 19 years, rather than seeking bigger and better – after all, he has many CEO years ahead of him.

For Mick, part of his 'call' has been to lead in a different way. Reflecting on his learning over the years he realised, 'All of my bosses, bar one, have been women, which was fairly exceptional in the late 1970s.' As a result he has made a point of recruiting women at all levels in Bromford, including senior management.

> This hasn't happened by accident. It's by having an open mind about the qualities and strengths they bring, both in terms of the hard stuff, and communication, sensitivity, awareness, appreciation of people and teamworking. Personally, I think one of the key strengths of this organisation has been its teamworking. I would say that generally speaking, openness, trust and teamworking are traits and characteristics that, all other things being equal, women do better than blokes.

What impact has that had on his style of leadership?

> I actually think you could argue a pretty convincing case for a CEO who does nothing else other than be positive and just encourage people, because out of that comes self-confidence and self-belief.

The same holds true for those leading any process or task – supporting and enabling your people is the main way to achieve the desired outcomes.

Emotional intelligence in leadership

The ability to connect with people at both head and heart level is one of the key strengths of high-performing leaders, according to Daniel Goleman in his work on *Emotional Intelligence*, and it is true that women tend to have high levels of EQ. The importance of people skills in effective leadership is born out by Mick.

> I believe it makes a difference to the business, but judge me on what we have achieved. We have grown well and the wheels haven't come off. We are measured as one of the best-performing associations in the UK. And we are making money.

Mick may sound a touch extreme, but he is in line with leaders at all levels in great companies. The first time I asked how much time was spent with people, as opposed to doing 'the leadership stuff', I was amazed to hear the reply '50 per cent.' I have continued to be amazed as that figure has varied from 50 per cent to 80 per cent. These are leaders who really believe that 'people are our greatest asset'.

It is a statement that makes clear the difference between management and leadership. As manager, the task is most important – to understand how it needs to work, who is to take which role, tracking progress, ensuring the outcomes. Once you move to a leadership stance, the emphasis moves to the people. A leader must still be ready to jump in and work with everyone else when the need arises, but there is a mindset shift – the job is to serve those committed to action on the task. To help them see the purpose, to keep their energy high, address their problems and concerns, and generally to care for them so that they can move forward.

What does 'spending time with people' mean?

Being available to talk is a major component, leading to open-plan offices, regular walks around the building, including satellite offices, instigating and taking part in fun events, working alongside people, and being on the end of the phone. In the traditional top-down command-control mindset it is strange to consider going for a chat with the 'royalty' CEO – it is such a palaver, why would you bother? Great company leaders are at work changing that mindset. Some even do all their own support work – Gary Hogan (of FC) looks after himself entirely. If you want an appointment with him, you call his mobile and arrange it with him direct, as you do with everyone else at Flight Centre.

This style of leadership takes the emphasis off the title – it is just another job in the team. As Mark Davies from Honda said, 'If I left, it would take six months for me to be missed. Others in the company would be missed immediately.' Everyone has their role and each is important to the well-being of the company. Leadership is not a matter of ego – or at least not just that: it is a matter of partnership, coupled with a desire to see other people fulfil their potential.

The importance of 'servant leadership'

There are as many ways to lead as there are people. For some it requires careful planning, developing the required business skills as their career progresses, and building the contacts and reputation. This produces some remarkable leaders. However, it does not always lead to the most exciting people cultures, and therefore not always to best development of the bottom line.

This is left to those leaders who develop themselves and want to see others come into their own. They want to lead people, rather than just have followers. This may seem like a hair-split – but it is the hallmark of what Jim Collins calls 'level-five leaders', and what Robert Greenleaf called 'servant leadership'. Level-five is one step up from a strong ego drive. The person is there to do a job that requires ego and leadership skills, but recognises that they will achieve nothing unless people choose to follow. And the way to encourage loyalty, followership and business effectiveness is through serving those who do the work.

Imagine, then, the impact on a business. A group of people working together, each striving to do their best, with the support and encouragement of leaders they respect and who respect them. Colleagues in these companies achieve more than they ever thought possible. CORGI takes on young adults who are having difficulty in finding a job. During three months of work experience they gain workplace and life skills that enable them to re-enter the job market with more of a chance. In fact, all have so far been invited to stay and are enthusiastically developing their careers in the company.

Keith is another wonderful example. He went to Bromford Housing Group as a temp and has just received his HNC and BSc in business information technology. Working with a servant leader who looks beyond first impressions, expecting there to be more than meets the eye, leads to all manner of discoveries.

Being a leader for money, kudos or control provides plenty of drive for success. Many have built strong and able organisations in just this way. However, they are always working within the limits of what they can imagine – they are the heart and author of the task. The business depends on their interest and initiative to thrive. The leader has built a concept, which other people have adopted and adapted to. Ideas that emerge from others will be measured against the concept and accepted or rejected accordingly. There is little room for development that does not fit into the prime mindset of the leader, with the limitation of their ability to imagine. Followers struggle when this type of leader moves on.

A servant leader has a mindset that is wider and more open to challenge or development. It is inclusive and encouraging of others – in fact, it depends upon them. The only limit is the imagination of the team. Using themselves as a vehicle, they can reach into new areas, opening up possibilities. No one person has all the answers, so accepting suggestions from every quarter is essential and increases the chance of success.

What is servant leadership and what difference does it make?
It is an unusual title and one that raises many an eyebrow. But just think for a moment about service. We look to excellent customer service as a way of supporting people to get what they need to move forward in their lives, whether that is going on holiday, buying a new house, getting a decent haircut or phoning directory enquiries. Companies known to give good service are highly successful. If service enables customers to move forward, why not offer the same to colleagues?

There are two distinct elements to the job of a servant leader:

- leading – understanding the bigger picture for the business, project, team – how the wider environment is faring and the impact this will have; customer needs; internal constraints and leverage; vision for the future. On-going assessment of this information leads to a picture of where to go in the future. A clear strategy is built around this understanding and conveyed clearly to the people concerned.
- serving – translating this direction is the next step of the process. The leader must build a picture so that colleagues can place their own work in the overall plan. For real involvement, people need to see the value, excitement and challenge of what they do. Command-control leaders tell. Servant leaders include, discuss, take ideas, look for ways to help people come on board, and celebrate every success that comes along.

Whatever your level in the business, the process is similar.

- Allocate half a day in a quiet space to think about your team in the context of the wider business. Develop a clear picture of the outputs required, overlaps and connections to other areas, contact with customers, and relationships with suppliers/ competitors.

- Build a plan of action taking all these elements into account. Include specific success measures. Be clear about the elements that are non-negotiable and what could develop through discussion with the team.
- Call a team meeting to communicate your vision and plan to your team. Present your ideas and then open up the discussion. Your people do the work each day – they will have good ideas about the best way to move forward. Enabling this conversation and taking on the most appropriate ideas will build ownership and show respect
- Ask how you can help them do the best job. Be prepared to give what is needed. This is not a 'one-off' question – you must keep asking and looking for ways to help and support. Challenge them to do a better, different, more effective job, and put the necessary support behind it.
- Help them build the competence necessary to do a good job, and trust them.

What great leaders actually do

The people I met all lead in their own way, yet are remarkably similar in philosophy: listen to everyone, pinch ideas from anywhere, trust those who do the job. In Honda it is ridiculous to tell people how to do their jobs. They are the ones who know. Having a conversation and looking for the way forward together is the only way to go. Asda had already pinched the best ideas from Wal Mart before they became part of the empire, and Wal Mart have now pinched some back in their new form. Timpson will always listen to ideas – in fact, they encourage everyone to try new ideas and pass them on when they prove effective.

We are looking at leaders who lead for their own sake and for the sake of those who follow. It sounds high-flown, and they have probably never consciously thought of it in that way – this is the magic of the outside view. Their high EQ is fundamental to their success, taking the organisation forward to bigger and better things. So how does this work?

Take Gary Hogan at Flight Centre. He and his colleagues have lost none of the entrepreneurial approach they used to create the company. 'Common sense before conventional wisdom' is the rule: if something is not working, they fix it. 'We've never had an original idea in our lives. Everything that works well we pinched.' Underpinning the success of the company is the belief that others will access that entrepreneurial energy if the environment is right. So Gary's job as leader is to enable people to discover and develop their potential, while having a great time and achieving what they want in life. Taking his own experience, he has built a way of leadership that brings out the best in FC people.

Understanding yourself and how you function is the starting point of EQ. We all see life through our own experience. It forms how we interpret the world and creates the mindsets that give order and meaning to life. The wise leader recognises that their view is just that – a view. No one else will see things in exactly the same way, so building an understanding of their mindsets, how they formed and how effective they are is the first step to being sensitive to the needs of others.

Common to great company leaders is this drive for learning. Personal development, coaching, feedback, benchmarking, reading, exploring new ideas are all ways of understanding how they influence the environment for good or bad. There is always more to be done, always the desire to move forward in a positive way. These are people who know they do not have all the answers. The moment I hear someone say that they do not need personal development, I know I am not dealing with a great company leader.

Tony DeNunzio had to find his own style of running Asda when he took over from Archie Norman. He knew he could not be the same, so it was an exploration to discover his own way of being CEO. He describes himself as

> conductor of an orchestra. I can tell them when they are out of tune or out of time with each other, and I can say when they are playing the wrong movement for the time. But they could play the symphony without me. I keep them on track, but they could work anyway.

However each person chooses to lead, there are common themes. Relationships sit right up front; understanding what makes people tick, what matters to them, what they want from life; taking the time to chat and find out about the recent holiday, how the kid's birthday party went and whether mother-in-law is feeling better. Frequently colleagues talk about the time their senior came and perched on the desk for a chat. Walking around the office with Bob Henry from CORGI, it was obvious that he was just one of the team – no one turned a hair. James Timpson has the phone numbers of his managers at his fingertips with no need to look in a diary. Such commitment builds self-esteem and trust – their behaviour states clearly that the person is important.

And this dovetails into another theme – that of being 'other-centred'. Personal development builds understanding and then enables attention to be turned outward to the rest of the team. Providing a nurturing, stimulating environment that develops self-esteem and confidence will open up ideas, exploration and progress. Seeing people grow and blossom is a major perk of leadership. And when that also leads to a positive change in the process or a new line of business, it is also a perk for shareholders.

Working so much with people will bring up all manner of personal reactions. How do you cope when:

- the person you believe in and promote is just not up to the job?
- you are sympathetic about time off and the person takes advantage?
- you arrange a celebration and most of the team do not attend?
- the piece of work you delegated goes to your own boss in a poor state and you are hauled over the coals?

However good your intentions, sometimes it will not work. That is to be expected and will provide huge learning. So you have to pick yourself up and look at the mitigating circumstances and your own contribution to the problem. Unless you take the learning, the same things will happen again.

- Talk with your HR department about personal and leadership development.
- Look at external courses so you can benchmark against other leaders and other companies. This will show where you can improve further.
- Take on a coach to help you understand your own behaviour in relation to your people. Couple this with 360-degree feedback to clarify your impact.
- Work out a specific plan of action to be tracked with your coach over the next six months to a year, and then repeat the 36-degree feedback to determine success.
- Keep some form of development going over time to ensure that you are making the best of yourself and those who work with you.

Mick Kent at Bromford sees the leadership development undertaken by the top team as a major factor in their success. That they are always stretching is a strong statement and role model in the company.

You must stay up to date with new thinking and changes in your work area, since this is constantly driving business forward:

- Choose an appropriate newspaper with a strong business section and read it each day or go on the Web each morning to find out what is happening. Read articles as well as the daily news.
- Subscribe to a relevant magazine that will keep you up to date with new ideas and company case studies – your HR department will have back copies you can choose from.
- Find out about interesting conferences and attend at least one a year. This will give you direct experience of new thinking, while building a network of contacts from other companies. You will learn a huge amount over coffee discussions, so do not sit on your own – go out and chat with people.
- Stay in touch with your network. Arrange one lunch a month with someone from another part of your business or an external in a similar job. Use it as a learning opportunity through swapping ideas and thoughts about the work.
- Find out about your local chamber of commerce or business forum and attend breakfast briefings with speakers who interest you.
- Ask HR if they know of leadership forums you could join – this is an excellent way of learning with a consistent group of people.

Being a strong role model is the main tool of servant leadership – behaving as you would have others behave and as the principles demand. However, it does not mean being a paragon of virtue. Servant leaders are as human as the rest of us. The difference is that when they mess up they acknowledge it and apologise, which is in itself a contribution to great company culture. Using themselves as an instrument, as a model of what is right for the work community, is a powerful tool. Words can go so far in persuading; what is actually done is far more influential. So demonstrating care of self, care of others, self-development, creativity, excitement and enthusiasm will have the greatest impact of all.

Summary

- Do not leave leadership to those with the smart titles. True, they are the ones with the 'helicopter view' that leads to great vision and strategy. But everyone has to be prepared to take the leadership opportunities as they arise – build on ideas, inspire others, motivate and align people to the vision.
- Connecting to the heart as well as the head is central to good leadership. Behaviour that shows people how important they are is an inspiration in itself.
- Servant leaders are inclusive and take their place in the team. Serve colleagues well, and customers will benefit.
- Great leaders discover their own style, keep learning, and develop strong relationships throughout the organisation.

What is the job of a leader?
Bob Henry (CORGI)

'To be available when someone wants to speak to you, whatever your role. Listen carefully and trust them to know their own job better than you – even if you used to do it yourself.'

Bob believes that the answers to every question are in the company, and so makes himself available for conversation. Once a concern is clarified, he encourages people to find a solution. If it is relevant, he'll be part of it; otherwise, he trusts them to do a good job.

This requires him to be fully available and Bob found an interesting solution. Above the reception area is a mezzanine floor – a grand way of describing the landing at the top of the stairs. He settles down here for the day, just him, his laptop and phone plus a table and chairs for 'entertaining'. Most people pass this way – not least because the loo is near by – so there are numerous opportunities for a talk.

'I am not switched on to general noise. I only notice when the tone changes.' When a disgruntled customer arrived in reception, Bob trusted it would be handled well, so just listened as the complaint was handed to the relevant person to sort out. Despite a good outcome, the customer persisted in complaining to the point of 'wanting to speak to whoever answers for God around here'. At which point Bob looked down from on high, saying 'You'd better come up then!'

Once the customer had got over the surprise of hearing 'God speaking from above', he accepted Bob's invitation to explore his concerns over a cup of tea. This resulted in a satisfied customer, with a clear understanding of why CORGI had acted in the way it had, and Bob got some useful customer viewpoints that he would otherwise have missed. His belief is that the conversation you miss or avoid is lost forever, as is the opportunity to gain the wisdom that would have emerged from it.

Bob's unusual leadership style has raised trust levels in CORGI. People take full responsibility, backed by support when requested. But how do you develop this level of trust as a leader? It requires faith in human nature and the recognition that everyone will do a good job, given the chance.

Many procedures are built around not trusting people, yet if you trust them you are rarely disappointed. I have been disappointed – of course I have – and it hurts on a personal basis, but you just have to deal with it. Breach of trust is fundamental and it can make it difficult for that person to stay with the business, in which case they need to move on. But you can't go through life being wounded, assuming everyone else is going to be untrustworthy.

Problems are identified and handed over to those most affected, because they are most likely to know what needs to happen. The call goes out for volunteers from the team or secondments from another part of the company, and the group comes together to understand the issues and search for next steps. Only those with a true interest get involved and the outcomes are highly effective. Both major and minor changes have been made in this way, and Bob has been less and less involved. End result – a committed workforce, skilled in problem-solving and motivated to give the best service to clients.

Action steps

Getting the best out of your people puts you ahead of the crowd. Remember: they are your competitive edge, the one thing others cannot copy. Create a positive, encouraging environment and you will maximise the talent your people bring to work each day.

Trust in your team

- Consider how willing you are to trust. If you find you are not, talk with your coach or a suitable colleague and try to understand why. Work out what needs to happen for you to change your behaviour.

- Make sure you are trustworthy: keep your promises, answer queries in reasonable time, keep confidences, treat people with respect. When you make a mistake, own up and apologise.

Encourage answers from the team
- Make a list of concerns about your area of the business. Choose one that will make most difference if sorted out.
- Identify the person most concerned with the issue. Meet and discuss the issues from different angles to understand their perspective.
- Send an invitation to the team and interested others, inviting them to join an exploratory discussion. Give a clear brief and state the purpose as seeking new ways of thinking.
- At the end of the meeting, ask for volunteers to form a steering group. Give a clear timeline for reporting back to the discussion group.
- Stand back and give support when requested, or take your place as an equal member of the team.

What is the job of a leader?
Liz Walford (Bromford Housing Group)

Everyone has responsibility for company culture. Tell stories about successes and mistakes, celebrate success and challenge, keep people in touch – this is the task of everyone who cares about the company.

Liz is often described as 'Keeper of the Flame'.

This means paying attention to the culture, our standards and what we mean by excellence. It means asking the question 'Is this good enough?' Sometimes it is, but sometimes it might mean saying 'We need to get this better, folks,'

With her wide responsibility for all operational and central support services, Liz is able to take an overview of the Group's work. She builds internal networks, as she can see who has information that will benefit another part of the business. 'I just prompt, nudge, encourage them to get in touch', and with that act, she maximises learning in the organisation.

She appreciates just how hard

people work and constantly reminds them 'what we are about as a business – our main objectives and our main statement of why we are here; helping by flagging up ways to see the wood from the trees.' Once a leader has set the direction, it is vital to keep people on track. With the weight of tough deadlines and challenging customers, gentle reminders of purpose become a necessity.

Liz heard someone speak about the 'tribal tales' of an organisation and the important role they play in maintaining culture. Although she does not see herself as a natural storyteller, Liz realised the importance of keeping history alive through stories, and so has practised the skill. Stories reaffirm the roots of an organisation, explain the need for particular principles and mark the successes and failures. We have these stories in families, friendships and companies. They help people understand us. That is why exchanging stories is such a regular feature of early relationships. Similarly, we become part of an organisation and really feel we belong when we know about its past. It helps us see where we fit in.

Great companies live by their principles and culture. Without the stories, new people will hear the words at induction programmes, but will not get the feel. The ideas will reach their brains but not their hearts – which is where culture really begins. So Liz is looking to become a better storyteller, modelling the principle of ongoing learning and keeping the flame alive in one go.

Action steps

Tracking workflow

- Set aside 30 minutes to think about the people who work for you. Note how energised and involved they are in their work. Identify ways you can help them do their job better.
- In your next one-to-one, remind each person of the business context for their work, how it fits into the business and how it affects the bottom line. Help them prioritise those tasks that have greatest impact on the business.

Company stories

- Do you know the stories of your organisation? If not, find someone who can tell you about the history, turning points and significant characters, and what can be learned from them.

- Use stories as illustrations. In team meetings and one-to-one sessions give examples of how people behave in the culture. This way you will keep ideas alive and increase your impact.

What is the job of a leader?
Mark Davies (Honda (UK))

'Build a picture, then help people see how they fit into it. Once they have this knowledge, they will see ways of making improvements.'
Mark Davies, general manager of the motorcycle business, claims that

> All I do is paint a picture. It is uncanny how human beings will progress towards the picture they have in their own mind. You don't have to dictate or tell. If the picture is compelling enough, people will mobilise themselves towards it. Once they are mobilised, you then coach them to see the value they add. Each person has to believe they are as valuable to that picture as every other individual.

During the last August issue of new number plates, when Mark was general manager of the car business, a team of five girls in logistics 'worked their socks off' as Honda sold 17,999 cars in the month. Knowing that dealers and customers would comment only on the 20 cars that were not delivered on time, Mark asked how they were feeling. He discovered that they did not recognise the significance of their contribution, despite sitting underneath a huge board which detailed performance – daily! So he sat down and coached them to identify the part they played. Finally, they saw that without their distribution skills the company would have sold significantly fewer than the magical 17,999.

> They came out of that session on top of the world, having put what they do into the context of the business. Not only were they proud, they also became more involved in the business. They now take ownership in a very different way.
>
> Every day someone will walk through the doors with a thought of 'bloody daft that we do things that way'. My job is to find ways of unlocking the knowledge and ideas that people don't articulate, in order for the business to improve. Put any two people together and they will have higher intellect than me and you can be sure they'll have an opinion. If the opinion is wrong, it doesn't matter. The one time they are right, you improve the

---

business. It is really dangerous to assume that people at different levels of the business have a higher or lower contribution to make, especially if they have the right attitude.

Mark knows when to listen and when to coach. He spends 80 per cent of his time 'paying attention' to what is going on around him and he claims that that is not enough. In Honda, everyone is expected to be a leader and take responsibility for their part of the business, bringing forward ideas and suggestions on how to improve. That is a great system and makes for a forward-thinking, creative environment – just what Mr Honda advocated. However, it works only because every leader is looking for that sparkle – or lack of it – and acting in full support of the next experiment.

Action steps

You need a clear and exciting picture of your work and how it fits into the business:

- If you are not clear, talk it through with your boss. If still not clear, go further up the organisation until you understand.
- Develop an exciting picture of your work and that of your team/colleagues.
- Use every opportunity to share the picture with your peers and direct reports – make sure you do this at least four times a day. Make it real by aligning it to each aspect of work in progress.
- Celebrate success, and demonstrate how it takes the work forward.

What is the job of a leader?
John and James Timpson

'Give responsibility and be present. Listen and question, but don't take over. Trust the people who do the work, but let them know you are involved. At every level, support those who work with you to do the best job they can.'

Life at Timpson is very down to earth.

We just help people do their job better, so they can earn more money. That's why people come to work – to earn money, not because we're lovely people, they have their birthday off or we send them champagne. But if you can make it good when they're there, that helps.

John and James lead in a way that is both hands-off and highly visible. 'We go to every shop at least once a year. We also go out with the area managers every year, often totally unannounced. For better or worse most people know who we are.' Since the time of writing, Timpson have bought the Sketchley group, and so now have 800 shops, but they still intend to visit as many as is humanly possible.

This could be seen as controlling, but managers have a high level of autonomy in how they run their shops.

It is important not to hand over authority, then go off fishing. That would be a disaster. We know a lot about the detail of the business, but rarely look at figures. We create a relaxed atmosphere, but have tight control. We know what the bank balance is every day, and exactly how much money each shop makes each month. Each week we get a detailed breakdown by department and shop, but don't often look at it – we already know it.

The end result is colleagues who take full responsibility for their particular part of the business, knowing they are well supported.

The basic philosophy is to get the best people, point them in the right direction and let them get on with it.

It is a blindingly obvious conclusion. If we want to amaze our customers, we are entirely dependent on the people who are in the shops now. So we trust them and give them authority. We always trust them to do whatever they think right to look after the customer.

Action steps

The most common mistake when giving responsibility is to abdicate. John and James Timpson avoid this by staying in touch with their people and ensuring that they know the state of the business day to day.

- Make a list of the work you have delegated, plus projects undertaken by your team. Write down all you know about the work – ie, is it on time? Is it delivering the required results? Is information being given to relevant people? Etc.

- At the first opportunity, speak to your people and fill in the gaps.
- Devise a procedure to ensure that you have the information you need in the future. Agree how this can be achieved and the regularity of reporting required. Look for a balance that keeps you informed without taking responsibility away from the individual.
- If you see figures/outcomes that concern you, *do not take over*. Make sure you understand the situation fully – what is working well, what is working less well, and how the person plans to go forward. Help them see the implications of their choices, and consider alternative ways forward if necessary. Support them in taking the work on to the next stage. If you take control, the person will never learn and you will retain the responsibility.

Lead by example

The stated principles and aims of a company are often mismatched with actual behaviour. Great companies go out of their way to make the cliché live – they 'walk the talk'.

If you have attended a presentation skills course recently, you know that only 7 per cent of communication is through language. We convey most through our behaviour, demeanour and body language. Makes you think, doesn't it? All those wise words you use to your colleagues, team or company mean nothing if your behaviour does not match up.

At Flight Centre, Gary Hogan, MD, demands that

> We lead by example – there are no administrators or secretaries of any kind. You have a measurable role and you perform in that role. In a shop you lead by example. We changed titles from 'manager' to 'team leader' to make that point. Lead by example in everything – the way you dress, the way you talk to customers, the way you treat your staff.

This is not an easy 'ask' – acting on wise words is very demanding. However, it is also satisfying and productive. Think of leaders you have known whose behaviour is out of line with their stated principles – my guess is you feel cynical as you recall them. Yet leaders who have shown integrity and truly 'walked the talk' will have gained your respect.

John Crabtree, senior partner of Wragge & Co., told me of a time when he encouraged the lawyers to share out work. Normal practice was to behave like a sole trader and do the work you were handed. He wanted the firm to develop experts who built relationships in their chosen field. He told his colleagues to 'think of the firm, rather than behave like Burglar Bill'. Fine words, but how did he feel when the next interesting piece of work landed on his desk? It was a tough moment – it looked exciting and challenging and he really wanted to do it himself. So he picked it up and walked down the corridor to the specialist colleague and handed over the brief.

That one act was the strongest message he could have given in support of the change he espoused. His message to the team was unequivocal, the best way to encourage others to follow the plan. The company is now known for its experienced business sectors specialists, which has proved to be a strategically sound move.

Do not bother with strategy meetings, business plans and cascades unless you are prepared to truly embrace the change yourself. People will follow what they see, not what they are told – so clean up your own act if you want to be a change agent.

Action steps

- Think of one person who is a role model for you: identify what you admire about their style/work. What would cause you to change your mind? How does your own behaviour match up?
- Look back over your day and identify three times when you lived to the principles and three times when you did not. Go back to those people who were affected by your lapses and apologise, providing a positive role model for how to handle mistakes. Make sure that you do not repeat the same behaviours a second time.
- Allow 10 minutes at the beginning of team meetings to give each other feedback on living the principles. Appreciate the positive and challenge unacceptable behaviour.
- When the team meeting is too public a place to confront some issues, use the one-to-one sessions with direct reports to give feedback and suggestions for improvements.
- Once the standard is improved, celebrate at the team meeting.

Chapter 5

Communication: creating colleague engagement

When was the last time you really listened to someone you work with? I am not talking about asking a question to evoke the answer you are looking for or writing an e-mail while another person speaks to you. I mean *really* looking, listening and sensing what the person is trying to communicate.

True communication builds a bridge between two people or within a group via which real understanding and contact occur. Martin Buber talks of the 'I-Thou moment' – the experience of being fully connected and open to the other person. It is the moment we covet in romantic relationships, but it also occurs in highly effective teams at their most creative, and between a great manager and colleague when information and thoughts are flowing.

A great company strives constantly towards this level of communication, through a desire to engage each and every person. Regardless of position, everyone has knowledge and ideas to add to the pot. By listening and sharing freely, people feel valued, involved, committed, and thereby raise the quality of the business output.

What is communication?

Communication enables every aspect of great company culture. Excellent leadership and management are built on it, belonging is evoked through it, and customer service depends upon it. It is also the source of creativity and innovation. Can you afford not to take a look at how effective you are?

The dissemination of information

Most companies are very good at this part of the process, ensuring that facts about the business, HR processes and benefits are available to those who need them. Impressive intranets allow everyone to access the details they need when they need them. Company magazines bring people up to date with changes, happenings and sometimes colleague stories.

AstraZeneca's Charnwood research and development site has a thorough and easily accessible intranet. Like everyone else, they had to grapple with the pull of the daily workload over staying up to date with happenings in the company. They have addressed this by creating an exciting and attractive front page that comes up when a colleague logs on in the morning. By constantly renewing this with information, news and questions, they encourage people to take a quick look at least once a day.

In most companies, information comes down at regular intervals from senior leaders, passed through the ranks by managers. Ideally, this is done on a regular basis to ensure that everyone is up to date with business changes, however small. Even when the news does not directly affect them, people appreciate the intention to include them. Wise companies put colleagues at the front of the queue when major change is about to hit – woe betide the leader who allows news to break in the press before they have told the staff!

The byword at Asda is 'communicate, communicate, communicate'. They know that it takes more than one pass for information to be taken in, so they repeat and reinforce what is being said in any way they can. David Smith, HR director, believes it is best to overdose on communication, making sure that everyone feels involved and included.

A company intranet is important and excellent when it works well. However, it is remarkably easy for those in positions of influence to tick the box when time and money has been spent on the right kit, without checking on effectiveness. I have heard far too often of smart intranets, only to hear that colleagues cannot all access a computer or just do not have time to read it.

So take the time to check how often people access your intranet. Ask questions and find out what will make it easier for them to remain up to date.

Company magazines work well when aligned to their customers. There is a danger in giving the task of production entirely to the PR or communications department. It will do a great job of producing a high-quality product appropriate to the brand. However, for some organisations, hearing about who has had a baby and the fun run completed by the accounts department is more important than glossy news from head office. Timpson produce a 36-page newsletter every Wednesday – not at all smart, but a great way of celebrating the high performers each week and passing on gossip. Even better, most of the news items are written by the staff themselves.

Part of the art of communication is to check how well your message has been received. So take the time to find out whether your company magazine is what people actually want. Do they read it and send in contributions? If not, why not? Ask them what will make it more interesting.

Management cascade

The management cascade is an effective way for organisations to disseminate information. However, it can also be fraught with pitfalls, so it is worth taking a dispassionate look at the effectiveness of your system. Ideally, senior leaders give regular updates to their direct reports, who then pass on all the information briefly and give details where it relates to their area of the work. So the process goes on, until each and every person is up to date with the latest changes.

As long as managers can listen, understand and repeat the essence and flavour as well as the words, the cascade works well. But this is notoriously difficult to achieve, dependent on the willingness, skill and sensitivity of the conveyer, and can be a prime source of confusion. Some managers take the task seriously, understanding that a strong sense of belonging requires consistent inclusion. Why would people believe it is 'their' company if information is withheld? Others seek to hold on to the power of knowledge, keeping others in the dark, unconsciously or deliberately.

You can find out how effective you are at conveying information by checking what messages people take away from a cascade meeting. Do this by chatting to people at random and listening carefully to what is said. If different people have a different understanding, talk with your peers to ensure common practice. This will make a really useful discussion point for your next management meeting – how often do you each pass on information, how well are the messages getting across, and what can you each do to improve the process?

When information is particularly important, involve the significant leader directly. This gives a clear message that colleagues are as important as the news itself. Do this when you want to engage people's hearts as well as just give them information, and always think it through from their perspective. Remember: what seems insignificant on the scale of things at senior levels can be extremely important to those directly affected or concerned. Having the manager or leader address these things personally will help with clarity as well as showing respect.

Mick Kent takes this one step further and sends a weekly e-mail bringing everyone up to date, not only on the business but on things happening in his own life. Hearing how the CEO's new cat is getting on can make him much more approachable in tough times – after all, he is 'just Mick'.

Upward communication

Information that travels from colleagues upwards is at least as important as top-down communication. Yet it is the most frequently ignored. Get this process firmly in place and real communication begins. Great companies place enormous emphasis on two-way contact – those who actually do the work have ideas and answers that senior people will never access on their own. If I had ten pounds for every time a great manager has told me that they trust their people because they are the ones who are doing the job, I should be a very wealthy woman!

There are two main aspects to this: mechanisms for ideas and concerns to reach senior leaders, plus effective conversation and feedback between managers and direct reports. The latter must be the starting point, since it underlies so many other aspects of a great culture, and the ability for everyone to speak to 'the boss' direct has an enormous impact. At Asda anyone can send a suggestion through to the CEO as part of the 'Tell Tony' scheme, and at Flight Centre, Gary Hogan is always on the end of the phone.

People really appreciate the commitment this demonstrates and the respect it shows for them as part of the organisation. All these leaders see themselves as part of the team, and so have to find ways to encourage others to see them that way too. Being at the end of the line like other team members is one way of ensuring that this happens.

It is really hard to find the time this requires, and it depends entirely on making people a priority. Clearly Tony DeNunzio does not look at each suggestion that comes from a colleague – a team of people work full-time on that. But he does take an interest and is involved in responses to the good ideas. People accept this as necessary, especially when he is present in other ways, like turning up in a shop and working alongside everyone else at 3 pm 'rumble time', when it is all hands on deck to tidy up before the late afternoon rush.

If the CEO of 137,000 people can be part of the team, it is clearly possible, as long as you make it important enough. Your door may very well be open – but do people actually walk through? When you take time with people, how effective are you at making a connection? If you have already looked ahead at the Timpson test in Chapter 6, check your scores. Just saying you are available and interested is not enough: you have to demonstrate it. And it is for you to do – do not expect others to take the responsibility when you are the boss.

Take every opportunity. Go for a drink after work, have a natter, talk about bits of your own life – let people know you, be interested and get to know them. It will pay off. The more involved you are, the more you will be included and the more likely you are to hear about ideas and concerns.

'I can look at this for myself, but how do I persuade more senior people to change their ways?'

Step one: beginning with yourself and your colleagues
Whether you have one direct report or a large division to care for, how you respond to people matters.

Make a note of how often people come to talk through ideas, concerns, and suggestions with you. If it is not happening:

- Chat briefly with members of your team each day. In your conversation include something of your life outside work (you do not have to share more than you want to, but knowing the person behind the role is a great for relationship building).
- Get to know people who are not in the immediate team – if you encourage a relationship, people will talk to you in return.
- When you hear of issues, go direct to the people concerned – in Honda-speak: 'Go to the place'. Understand what the real concern is and ask how you can help. People will see that you really are interested, and so will talk to you in the future.
- When someone does come to talk, take time to listen. Everyone will watch your response – the word gets round like wildfire, so making it a positive experience will reinforce that you mean it.

Keep a note of how this behaviour impacts on the effectiveness of your team. As soon as you see signs of positive change, move to the next step.

Step two: influencing in senior places
If you already work in a positive workplace, it is likely that managers and leaders will appreciate hearing that they are not available enough or that people hang back from talking to them. All it needs is for you to have the courage to tell them. If it is difficult, enlist the help of your manager or someone in your network who is more familiar, or write a note or e-mail.

If this is not in the culture of your company, you have to find a way to influence thinking at senior levels.

- Begin where you feel comfortable – use your own experience and talk with your peers about the advantages of getting feedback and ideas from people they work with. Tell them how you made this happen; encourage them to do the same. Suggest a time at the beginning of your peer team meetings to share good ideas.
- As a team or group of peers, keep track of the benefits. When you are ready, take your learning to those at the next level. Use as much tangible evidence as you can, highlighting how ideas and concerns have improved outputs or achievement of targets.
- Talk about what great companies do – use evidence from this book and the *Sunday Times* list to demonstrate the positive impact of such behaviour.
- Encourage your managers to talk to those above them about the benefits.
- Do not expect instant change – incremental development will be much more effective. Keep speaking of your team's achievements: it will be great for them and will also spur people's interest so they want to know what you are doing.

Building critical mass is the main way forward. It takes time and courage, but will also be extremely rewarding. The relationships you build will stand you in good stead for years to come, and the commitment in your team will increase as they realise you really are interested.

Communicating the vision

A lot of companies do the vision exercise, tell everyone about it, and then return to their old ways. Talk vision and values, and eyes begin to glaze over. There have been too many expensive exercises making little tangible difference for the topic to be taken seriously. Yet a positive and exciting picture of the future gives people something to get out of bed for. Without it, life is what we do when we have finished work.

Passion and heart are words not often used in business, but this is what has driven excellent businesses since time immemorial. Great innovators, inventors, entrepreneurs are driven by their passion for a product, money, a service, or success itself. All business has been started by one or two people on a mission. There are endless stories of entrepreneurs who ended up running big businesses – Hewlett and Packard, Bill Gates, Richard Branson were all driven by passion and dogged determination.

The start-up of a new idea or business needs high energy, bloody-mindedness and the ability to keep going in tough times. It needs more than one person to have the passion. And as long as someone is positive and solid, it is possible to overcome the down times and keep going. This happens most easily when the business is small because people are influenced by the passion of the originator/idea, especially if the leader is charismatic and dynamic. In fact, it is so exciting that it can be hard to stay away.

This is a long way from the big blue-chip and public sector companies of today. But the basis is the same. Everyone needs to be touched by the passion – in fact, it is even more important at this level. At the beginning, work is exciting by virtue of its newness. Once the business is bedded in and running on rails, it can become humdrum. The excited leader has disappeared into the top office, to be seen only by the loyal few, and 'business as usual' is firmly planted. But it was passion that got this machine up and running, that made it exciting enough to work really hard. And it is passion that must keep it going.

An inspiring vision engenders this level of passion, and talking about it regularly keeps it fresh and new. This is a communication job for every manager. Think of yourself as an entrepreneur. If you do not inspire people to do a good job, who will? The work has to tap their excitement, has to get them thinking of new ideas, noticing how other companies work, feeling proud of what they do. Once you have this level of commitment, they will go to bed at night satisfied, believing in themselves and their work. And they will give the customers and company a really good deal.

Keeping the vision alive

Enthusiastic people activate an inspiring vision – but only if they have regular encouragement. The vision must be restated, consistently reminding people why they are doing the work, why it matters to the company, customers and themselves, and to stimulate new ideas. A concept is alive only when people truly want to play their part.

It was Jack Welch who said that unless he spoke about the vision each day, he was not doing his job. Placing daily tasks in the context of the bigger picture is an effective way of validating what people do. This is how you move from bricklaying to building a cathedral.

The story of the person who described a wide, grey, scaly column without realising he was looking at the leg of an elephant is a wonderful way of describing most people's working day. They concentrate on the task at hand and ensure that they meet deadlines without seeing what they do as an integral part of the puzzle. Vision builds the big picture, encourages the heart and takes people forward to a more meaningful sense of their work.

Honesty

Communication and conversation are effective only when they are honest. True honesty is relatively rare because it is hard to achieve. It is so much easier to say what a person wants to hear and only the brave want to hear the truth, so the tendency is to pull punches for the sake of an easy life.

One of my personal guiding themes is *harmlessness*. Imagine what life would be like if everything we did caused minimum harm to self and others. This is a major challenge that demands honesty, not only with others but also with yourself. There is no room here for the easy option. Telling an ineffective colleague that their work is good enough may be easy in the short term – it certainly avoids confrontation. In the long run it is harmful – the colleague settles for second-best and never discovers where their real talent lies; the team pick up the shortfall, lose confidence in the boss and maybe even leave; and the manager is left trying to manage an unhappy team with the inevitable kick-back on the bottom line.

True harmlessness means looking at each situation from the long- and short-term perspective. If an easy life now leads to distress or ineffectiveness in the long run, it is really not an option.

'What you see is what you get' is a frequently heard phrase, meaning 'I am forthright and will tell it as I see it.' Presumed to be a truthteller, in fact the speaker is more likely to be one who expects everyone else to accept their life view. This is not harmlessness.

Harmlessness is:

- acknowledging the truth as you see it – understanding how a situation impacts on you in your present situation and identifying the truth you believe should be told:
- being honest about your intentions – who will benefit/lose from what you have to say?
- looking at the truth from the other person's perspective – what is important? Why does it matter? What is needed? Then consider how your own truth looks from that other perspective – what will it achieve? Who will benefit? Who could feel damaged as a result? What is the most likely outcome for the business?
- looking forward to see what must happen to ensure that each person feels respected and that the outcome is most effective for the people and the business. What must happen now in order that this is achieved in the future?
- re examining your original truth – does it still feel like the truth, or are there other elements that must be added in? What is the action you actually need to take to ensure harmlessness in the future?

Lee, regional manager at Timpson, knew that a young man in one shop was arriving late for work on a regular basis. The manager had done his best, but nothing was persuading the young man that he must be on time. It was easy to understand – the draw of his first regular income and the resulting social life was too great. He did not want to see the consequences of his behaviour. Lee could have left it for a time, believing that he would settle down once the novelty wore off. However, this would risk a negative impact on the business and the safety of his job if he did not change. To do nothing was potentially harmful.

The first step was to buy him an alarm clock, but this had little effect. So Lee sat down with him and outlined the risks of continuing with the behaviour, including the worst-case scenario – 'You could lose your job.' This, coupled with the manager calling him at wake-up time for a few weeks, helped to embed a new pattern and he is now back on track. Facing the tough conversation led to a harmless outcome.

In a company I shall not name, I met Kelly (not her real name) who suffered from a bullying boss. Our discussion confirmed that the behaviour was not acceptable and that some action must be taken. Afraid to go to direct to the bully's own boss, she spoke to the HR department, who spoke on her behalf. But this was a tough situation – the difficult manager was a good performer. Known to be poor with people, his results were nonetheless exceptional and he did not like to be criticised. What should the boss do?

This is not an unfamiliar situation by any means, and a classic in the harmlessness stakes:

- Don't act, and the high performer will continue to deliver.
- Don't act, and the team members will either leave or take the path of least resistance, losing enthusiasm, excitement and commitment to the business.
- Don't act, and the word will get around that you condone bad behaviour and that colleagues are less important than the business.
- Act, and the high performer could take offence and reduce the effort he puts into work, or leave for pastures new where his behaviour will be accepted
- Act, and you give a clear message to colleagues that you do not condone inappropriate behaviour, increasing their respect and trust in you.
- Act, and the high performer may be prepared to change his behaviour, which could mean he takes his eye off the ball for a time, reducing his output.

Now look one year ahead:

- *If no action was taken*, you still have your high performer and the numbers are good. However, you have a high recruitment bill and a complaints procedure to deal with. Word in the company is that you care only for the bottom line, so commitment is down. What seemed like the easy option last year is now a major obstacle to the business.
- *If positive action was taken*, you may have lost your high performer, with the resulting loss to the bottom line as you looked for the right person and got them settled in. However, you have a strongly committed team who trust you to listen to them and honour their

concerns. They will go out of their way to deliver for you because they have respect for your courage and ability.

- *Or*, the high performer was deeply concerned to hear that he was being a bully. He had not realised the impact he had and was really keen to change. Because of his delight in numbers and delivery, he put people second. Coaching and management support has helped him begin to adapt his behaviour, and the team are right behind him.

There are pros and cons to each action, but it is clear that considering the long-term view is the only way to assess where greatest harm could lie.

Why not be honest?

It is not easy to tell the truth, and people avoid it for all sorts of reasons:

- fear of the unknown – Staying with your own picture of life brings a level of safety. Mindsets determine how we interpret events, leading to well-worn paths of behaviour. To step outside that tried and tested box is scary. To be open to comment from anywhere makes life unpredictable. Consider David Smith from Asda: all 137,000 colleagues are invited to comment when they want to. 'I get it thrown back at me the moment I don't live the values.' Under those circumstances, life is a challenging experience and not everyone is prepared for that level of honesty.
- fear of the tough situations – Real honesty requires a determination, tough spirit and adherence to principles that some are not willing to commit to. Situations like that of the bullying manager separate the successful from the great companies. Being principle-driven requires you to deal with even the thorniest situations, having an open mind and honest intent. And people may not like you in the short term.
- loss of power – Knowledge can be seen as power – something to be hugged to the chest for times of need. Honesty requires sharing for the good of the whole, ensuring that everyone has the information that enables them to do their job to best effect. Not only is the power shared, so are the successes. Being a team player means putting personal gain alongside company gain. You are great only when everyone is great. At Flight Centre and Asda, everyone knows how the company is doing. Figures for company and team are shared each week at Asda. At Flight Centre everyone has access to company

figures and is given training on how to read a spreadsheet to make sure they understand it. In Honda everyone is considered part of the team – no one role is more important than another. All this is great if you like to be part of a greater team. If you build your sense of self around your status or the knowledge you hold, this is a tough act to be part of.

The best output from a principles-based honest conversation is that all parties understand what the issues are, feel heard, maintain their self-respect and are able to act on decisions for the good of themselves and the business.

There are simple guidelines for such discussions, whether about clear business issues, personal development obstacles or underperformance:

- Take time on your own to plan:
  - Book a comfortable room for the meeting, where you will not be interrupted.
  - Understand the facts of the situation: find out by talking to everyone involved to get a balanced point of view.
  - Consider the outcomes you need. Is this one of a series of steps, or do you expect this to be sufficient on its own? What agreements do you need from the other, and what agreements are you willing to make yourself?
  - Give notice to the other person when you need them to bring specific information, if they need time to plan and think about their input.
  - If you believe warning of the subject matter may bring unnecessary worry to the other person, think it through carefully to make sure whether that really is the case. Discuss it with a colleague to get a second opinion. Consider how it will impact on the outcome and if it is appropriate.
  - Study your personal responses to the situation. How personally involved are you? Will the outcomes affect your work or reputation? Does the issue impact on your sense of integrity or your principles? Are you able to be objective? After an honest assessment, clarify whether you can handle the discussion alone or whether you need support or a mediator.
  - Identify any mindsets that might trip you up – eg assumptions you make about what is right or wrong behaviour. Clarify where these fit with company mindsets and where they are out of

kilter. Being conscious of this will stop you being pulled off course. If you think this is an issue, get some support.

- At the meeting:
  - Outline the agenda and where you want to get to.
  - Set some ground rules – eg clarify whether the subject matter is confidential, agree that people will not talk over each other, that people will be treated with respect, etc.
  - Set time boundaries, and stick to them.
  - Set the scene: describe the situation as you understand it, then ask each person to do the same.
  - Ensure that you listen fully to other accounts, asking questions to make sure you understand. Periodically, rephrase what has been said so that people can affirm that you have understood them – 'So what you are saying is . . .'
  - Remember: everyone's perception is true for them. Be honest about your own perceptions, work to understand theirs, and help them understand the impact of their behaviour, decisions or actions. This is where you must be honest. Make sure each person leaves understanding fully what they have been told.
  - Close the meeting with a summary of the points discussed. Write down agreed actions and any concerns going forward, to be distributed to those present. Agree who carries responsibility for which actions and the timelines involved.

- After the discussion:
  - Leave time for the information shared to settle in.
  - Make individual contact the next day to ensure that those involved are clear on the outcomes and the next steps.
  - Take the necessary steps to follow through on agreements made, and call the next meeting when appropriate.
  - Continue with honest conversation. Once you have set the tone, do not let it drop. Being a strong role model for honesty will be a positive force – this includes acknowledging when you have made a mistake or a poor decision. This will have a profound impact on others and encourage them to be equally honest.

Creativity

Honesty and respect create an environment in which people are prepared to make a mistake and risk looking silly – and this is where creativity and innovation thrive (see Chapter 6 and the section on managing mistakes). Exploring new ideas means going out on a limb, but it also means taking the risk that someone will laugh at or deride the idea. Strong people are unfazed by this possibility and go ahead anyway; others back away from it.

As a manager, your task is to make it safe to experiment. At first glance it can seem easier to accept everything and not rock the boat, but in the long term this leaves people feeling undervalued and unexcited. At St Luke's they talk about providing safety and challenge in balance – a tough task for managers and leaders. It means creating a 'safe emergency' – inviting people 'out of the box' while providing a safety net. If the net is too small, they will not play; if the net is too big, they will be too comfortable.

Your personality as a manager is a big driver in this – you must be trustworthy if you want people to take a risk around you. Be open with information, listen well, answer questions honestly, own up when you make a mistake, tell the truth, and show you care about the people who work for you. This example will build an atmosphere of open communication and be a positive driver for the business.

Summary

- Communication goes up, down and across in a great company.
- Be a positive example to those who work with you. This will encourage them to improve their own communication.
- Encourage other people to attend to their communication by your example. Look for evidence in your own experience that effective communication is good for the business.
- Keep the team/company vision in front of people: it is what engages their hearts as well as their minds.
- Be 'harmless' in your behaviour. Make sure that what you do will have a positive impact both now and in the future.
- Choose honesty over the easy option – it will pay off in the long run.
- Foster creativity by building trust. Develop a reputation for honesty to increase the safety of the environment.

Ideas for communication

Chatting to the senior partner in Wragge & Co.

Having access to senior people is an important element of great company culture. Colleagues feel included, valued and listened to. Equally, senior leaders get to hear what is happening in the business.

Some leaders remain at the top of the mountain, out of touch with what goes on below the cloud layer. They may feel safe, creating their own reality, but this lack of interest means they are disengaged from colleagues.

The senior partner of Wragge & Co. sits in a room all alone in order to communicate with everyone in the firm. That sounds odd, but it works really well. You may ask why he uses a live chat room when he could speak face to face. Yet the rationale makes sense: not everyone feels easy about having a conversation face to face with 'the boss' – it can seem too daunting. A computer screen is a different proposition altogether. Then people can be open, honest and pretty frank, it seems.

At regular intervals, John Crabtree sits in front of the screen, available for an afternoon of answering questions, listening to concerns and exchanging thoughts and ideas. The subject matter ranges from the state of the world through to the state of the local football team, passing through business issues on the way. People can maintain their anonymity if they so choose, but this is rare. The non-threatening nature of the medium leads to laughter, meaningful discussion and positive outcomes for colleagues and company alike.

A flag meeting at St Luke's

Sharing ideas, receiving feedback and getting encouragement are essential in creative organisations.

On the last Friday of every month, the whole company gathers in the restaurant at St Luke's for a 'flag meeting'. This is the chance to share the successes, disappointments and conundrums of the past weeks and to get some feedback. Each team shows the work they have achieved – new plans made, adverts designed and ideas that did not quite make it.

It is a great way to celebrate success, congratulating those who have won business or delivered exciting work to clients. Fun, exciting, but not easy. True success also requires the willingness to talk about what did not work and why. Flag meetings include this too – all ideas are presented, drawing comments from people who see the value – or not – in what has been produced. Suggestions are made, thinking is challenged, and everyone is placed on their toes for the month ahead.

Not everyone can manage this level of openness. You have to find the way that suits your people and your business – but the idea of an open forum that assesses work is an interesting one. When done with a care and concern that is both challenging and supportive, it is a real spur to excellence.

Timpsons' area managers conference
As soon as you bring people together good ideas can flow. Two heads are always better than one.

Where people travel and work in isolation it is hard to keep them engaged. At Timpsons, individuals run shops, sometimes alone, serviced by area managers. These people travel the country providing the support and rigour needed to maintain the excellence that is central to the Timpson brand. Under these circumstances, keeping everyone aligned is no easy matter.

Every quarter, area managers come together for a meeting. To quote James Timpson:

John gives some figures for about 30 minutes and I take 20 minutes to talk through

two or three issues we have. The next step is to give a few awards to the best performers. Then it's out on the town and throw beer at them. I don't care if they're up until 5 in the morning – the most important time in manager's conference is when they talk to each other. Next day we put them in five groups of three and give them from two to three questions, like how to recruit more women or how to manage their time. They come up with ideas and present them back for 10 minutes. I write it all up, take the boards home, type them and send them out – that's all we do.

But they will start recruiting more women and improve time management. We did not tell them how to do it, because they came up with the idea. They are on the ground and teach each other, so it happens. That's our system.

Suggestions boxes at Richer Sounds
Answers are obvious when you work in an area every day. Not accessing that information is detrimental to the business.

When you work directly with customers you know first-hand what works well and what drives everyone mad. We all recognise the organisations that do not trust their staff, and as a customer it is deeply frustrating to stand and wait for a senior manager who wants us to begin all over again. It affects the tone of the contact with the company and can be a spur never to use them again.

At Richer Sounds, David Robinson, CEO, does trust those who work for the company and recognises the knowledge they hold. Asking for regular input, he is concerned if no comments or suggestions come through. If colleagues are working well and having a good time, they will automatically think of how to give a better service to customers. Knowing that the leadership needs to hear from them is a great spur to creativity and engagement – they really are part of the success of the company.

Honesty at Microsoft
It is all too easy for senior people to sit with their head in the clouds, especially if people cannot give honest criticism when mistakes are made. Managers and leaders must develop a culture of honesty or the business will suffer.

Steve Harvey has a challenge to all newcomers: 'If you see something and think it is stupid, tell me and we'll get rid of it.' That level of honesty takes some getting used to, but once accepted is a great way to move forward. What looks eminently sensible at the top of an organisation can clearly be a non-starter to those directly involved. Ensuring access is an excellent way to maximise sensible behaviour in a business.

In such an electronics-friendly environment, response is rapid. 'Any stupid policy will be thrown back at you in the first two minutes of being launched via e-mail on the Web. You get feedback pretty quickly about whether it is sensible or not.'

Action steps

There are two aspects to every system of communication:

- Does it work effectively?
- Will people use it?

You have to ensure that each element is in place.

- Consider the e-mail system:
- Encourage people to speak face to face whenever they can.
- Stop endless copying in for the sake of it.

- Instigate e-mail-free days.
- Give e-mail access to senior leaders. If the response is high, find someone who can screen the messages, putting the important ones in front of the person directly and attending to all the others.

Consider meetings:
- Encourage people to take ownership by trusting them to act.
- If this is not in the company ethos, set clear agreements about delivery and milestones.
- Share responsibility for running the meeting in order to increase engagement.
- Experiment with stand-up meetings to reduce the time taken.
- Put people into small groups so that everyone gets a chance to speak and discuss ideas.
- Invite criticism. Listen carefully to what is said, and act on it where it makes sense, or explain why you are not acting on it: this is the only way to ensure that you get the truth.

Consider how ideas may be generated:
- Try having a suggestions box system – but only if you are prepared to acknowledge ideas in a short space of time and give a full response as soon as possible.
- Bring people together to talk about the work they are doing and to exchange ideas.
- Encourage the giving and receiving of feedback by being open to it yourself.
- Have open forums to which people can bring thoughts, concerns, and problems for discussion with interested people.
- Have team meetings at which you discuss an issue in the business. Leave people to act on their ideas, giving them support when they need it.
- Always celebrate successful ideas and good tries as soon as you can.

Chapter 6

Management: the lifeblood of great company culture

'I was always taught to manage as if I was the host of a house party. Take care to make sure that people have what they need, that they are comfortable, talking to the right people and enjoying themselves. And it works for me.'

In her job at Kent Messenger, Viv is first port of call for rookies entering the newspaper business, since she gives them such a good start. By supporting their learning, challenging them to do a really good job and celebrating their success, she provides a great environment for them to excel in their early days. People who begin with such care are more likely to make great managers themselves in the future.

To quote John Timpson from his little book *How to Be a Great Boss*:

> Great bosses come in all shapes and sizes ... it's the person's personality that counts. A boss's reputation depends on his people – great bosses have great people. As soon as they think they are dispensable, they can lose the plot.

As John says, the team need the manager to make decisions, but it is the team that turn the decisions into success. This is the central thrust of great company management. Managers create the environment that will support, challenge and bring out the best in people.

So that phrase 'servant leadership' crops up again – and here we are talking not just about designated leaders but about everyone who works with people. John Timpson calls it 'upside-down management', Flight Centre talk of 'back-to-front leadership', but the impact is the same. In servant leader organisations, managers see it as their job to help people do their work well. And that is upside-down to many managerial mindsets. The power of the boss goes out of the window and the importance of the colleague flies in.

Once this happens, a different competence is required. When choosing managers, people skills take priority over specialist skills. So many scientists, engineers, teachers, accountants, etc are promoted into management roles because they are great at their work. They may be hopeless with people, but taking on management responsibility is the only way to move up the ladder. However, management is a skill in its own right – a fact readily acknowledged in great companies.

Companies like AstraZeneca have created a whole new career structure around scientific skill to ensure that this does not happen. They also recognise that highly skilled specialists are so good at the job because they love it. Take them away from the nitty-gritty and they lose their delight. Putting them with people to manage is not fair to them or to the business. Honda have done the same for management, having a small number of people who specialise specifically in management.

Get to know your people

Managers make decisions that affect people's lives every day of the week, and some of them do so with little true knowledge of the lives involved. What chance, then, is there of a successful outcome?

When new people come into a business it is customary to introduce them to how things work, to how they may gain acceptance and to what is expected of them. What is less common is for the manager to take time to understand what drives the new colleague and what is required of them as a manager.

Managers are pivotal in the workplace, as demonstrated by research that shows that 70 per cent of people leave their manager and not the job. Each manager or leader I spoke to in the great companies emphasised the significance of getting to know your people. The willingness and ability to perch on the desk on Monday morning and chat about the weekend plays a major role in the happiness and productivity of colleagues. Mark Davies at Honda resists the temptation to rush to sorting out e-mail, letters and the week ahead in order to hear the latest news. Instead, he makes his way slowly across the office, chatting as he goes – and clearly enjoying himself. He spoke with fascination about listening to Bob Angel talk about his Sunday spent repairing old Bakelite phones, which Mark describes as being 'works of art'.

As manager or colleague you would be well advised to find out about the people who work alongside you. I asked Steve, a shop manager for Timpsons, what he thought most important in managing the one person who works with him. 'Treat him like a human being,' was the answer. This may seem blindingly obvious, but it is a statement I have heard many times both from those who are treated in this way and those who are not. A sad statement, but true – too often colleagues are treated as performing numbers with little respect coming their way. One Timpson manager who has been recently 'acquired' by the company is thoroughly enjoying his new place of work because the managers are 'hands-on, friendly, and if we have a problem, they come straight out to help'. Lee, the regional manager, already understands that he needs to stay in touch – 'Leave him too long and his head will go down. This is not an easy shop to run, so he needs all the support he can get.'

Working as a manager carries vast demands, so the request to get to know all of your people and take time for a regular chat can seem like one too many. But remember the wise words of John Timpson: 'Great bosses have great people.' The minute your people under-perform it reflects on you, and more importantly, costs the business.

A popular misconception of managers is that they are not really that significant. Forget that one right now   to your direct reports YOU ARE A REALLY IMPORTANT PERSON. Do not for a moment underestimate the motivation created by you when you take the time for a chat. It is a basic statement of respect – letting people know that they matter to you. If you work in a hierarchical structure, the impact will be even greater.

What to do about it? Try the Timpson test. Mentally choose one direct report at random and answer the following. Add up the points for those you get right:

Do you know his or her	score available	your score
Age	5	
Address	5	
partner's name	10	
children's names/ages/schools	20	
last holiday	10	
next holiday	5	
main hobbies	10	
partner's hobbies	5	
career history	10	
skills diplomas	5	
health record	5	
make of car	5	
parents' names		
	TOTAL:	

If you score more than 70, you are a people person.
If you score less than 70, get to know your staff better before taking the test again.

The manager as talent scout

Apart from the marked human impact of knowing your people and showing you care about them, it is a vital part of developing potential. How can you expect to get the best out of people when you do not know what matters to them, what their ambitions are or the areas of work that excite them?

Every business needs people who are hungry for change and development. The present business environment is not one for shrinking violets who want life to remain the same. Great companies have learned the value of 'grow your own' – they recruit mostly at entry level and grow their future senior leaders and managers in-house. Apart from the obvious benefit of upskilling in just the way the company needs, the positive impact on sustaining and building the culture is enormous.

Colleagues must demonstrate their talents, but managers have a responsibility to pay attention so that none of that ability is lost to the organisation. Because not everyone is willing to shout from the rooftops, the manager must know each person well, their style of relating, their interests and career aspirations. Just think back to a time when your manager took your ambitions seriously and how much that meant to you – now it is your chance to return the favour.

And the benefit is not only to the individual. When you identify potential and develop a team of great people, not only will you gain a reputation to match but you will also have a true team that can take some of the work off your desk; which will give you the time to get to know them even better; which will mean you can develop them well, and so on, and so on . . .

This brings us to the thorny question of delegation and those oft-heard cries:

- 'I don't have time and they don't do it as well as me – it's quicker to do it myself.'
- 'This "pie in the sky" idea of coaching is just not reasonable to expect. I have too many other demands to cope with.'
- 'My managers are shouting for action, so I just keep my head down and get on with it.'

Sound familiar? These are cries I have heard many times over the years, and I do know how tempting it is to just 'do it yourself'. But in the long run it does not work. You get burnt out, your good people get frustrated and leave you or the company, and you end up with exactly what you believe you had in the first place – a team that is not able to do the work. It is called wish-fulfilment.

If you are going to be a great manager, you need to be a talent scout as well as delivering results, and the two go extremely well hand in hand.

What to do?

Go for a walk and do some thinking.

From a distance, take a good look at the 'game' of business. The main players are people – unless they choose to play, the game does not exist. From this perspective give some thought to your direct reports – without them your piece of the business would not exist. That is how important they are.

Then take a good look at yourself. Are you willing to give up some

control and let people make mistakes? If not, get back to your desk
– you have an awful lot of work to do!

Make a list of the people in your team, together with their skills,
latent talents, and ambitions.

For example:

Name	Present role	Skills	Latent talent	Ambition	Potential
Mary Smith	Secretary	well organised, good manner, keen to develop, enthusiastic, perceptive	leadership, work directly with people, challenging, a people champion	HR work, learning/ development, management	delegate HR liaison, utilise organisational skills more effectively

Set aside time with each person and identify their ambitions, how
excited/frustrated they are at present, and what their ideas are for
improving the team output. Check how your assumptions fit with
theirs.

Map aspirations against the demands of the team and see what it
would look like if you gathered all the talents together.

Call a team meeting and put forward your ideas to date. Have a
discussion about options and ideas, including them in the next steps.

Follow-up
Having found out about possible areas of talent, ambitions and
hopes, you must follow through. Just listening is not enough – you
will build up hopes only to dash them again, and it is hard work to
retrieve yourself from that sort of let-down. So:

- Be on the lookout for challenges you can hand on.
- Ask each person to create an action plan, identifying the skills that
  need development if they are to move forward. Involve each individual in seeking out ideas for how to address these.
- Give time to coaching and/or arrange for an appropriate mentor
  from within the company or team who can pass on skills and tips
  from their own experience.
- Be prepared to support through new experiences, having one-to-
  ones at regular intervals – ie at least once a month – to make sure
  all is going well.
- Remember not to 'hand over and go fishing', as John Timpson says
  – delegation involves care, support and challenge, not abdication.

Managing mistakes

When people stretch to hone their talents, they are sure to make mistakes. This is an important part of success, but only when every effort is made to learn from the bits that go wrong. Everyone makes mistakes – even you. After all, you are only human. Great companies regard mistakes as par for the course and part of the learning process. Think back to a mistake you made – I bet you never made it again.

Responding in a positive manner when something goes wrong is a skill in itself. This is where trust comes in. Understanding that no one makes a mistake on purpose will calm your thinking, giving enough time for the person to explain. Remember those times of practising over and over again how to own up, hoping you will get it all out before your manager hits the roof – unhappy times, indeed! Punishment ensures that the colleague will never take a risk again – so no more mistakes, but no more creativity either.

Listen, empathise, explore how the mistake occurred, and look for alternative responses for the future. Be the 'grit in the oyster', using every tool to help development. Validate the desire to do a good job and you will gain trust and commitment beyond measure. What has happened may well be the best training available. These mistakes rarely happen again, but if they do, more decisive action needs to be put in place to understand if it is a lack of capability or lack of commitment. Both must be addressed.

When developing people is a management objective, using mistakes is just one way to extend knowledge and understanding. On-going appraisal maximises learning by considering actions and their outcomes. Doing this regularly is the only way to make sure that all avenues are covered. This is why many of the great companies hold appraisals or regular one-to-ones each month at least. (See Chapter 8.)

Of course, appraisal ideally goes both ways. Who better to say how a manager is doing than those who report in? When feedback is two-way, the manager can improve their own style while learning how to support the direct report more effectively. At Flight Centre, the manager's manager looks for ways to further develop the team leader by speaking to each team member once a month. In many companies this would be frowned on for contravening the hierarchy – it is difficult to 'go round your manager' to speak to someone more senior. However, the gains are enormous, if challenging and a bit on the scary side.

Keeping people motivated and energetic is not always an easy job, so the more support a manager gets, the better.

Right person, right job

Which brings us to a central tenet of a great company: put the right person in the right job. It sounds so obvious and simple, yet it is often not the case. A prime task of managers is to ensure that their people are well utilised, and this requires good knowledge of the individuals who work in the team.

How many people do you know who are struggling to do a job? Most readers will be able to think of at least one person, and the end result in most cases is under-performance.

There are a number of possible reactions to this situation:

- Set the person clear deadlines and objectives, then meet regularly to support them through discussion and appropriate coaching.
- Ask HR to provide the necessary training and development.
- Consider other jobs – a 'problem person' in one team can be the star of another.
- With the backing of HR, work towards moving them out of the company, explaining exactly why it is necessary.
- Get the team to pick up the shortfall, so that no one has to face an uncomfortable discussion.
- Find a backwater job where they will not cause too much damage.

Unfortunately, the last two options are all too frequently taken up, especially in successful companies where behaviours are not congruent with the principles. The real problem is that people back off from telling the truth.

> It is really hard to tell someone that they are not doing a good job. But how hard do you think it is knowing that *you* are not doing a good job? Remember: everyone wants to go home at the end of the day with a sense of satisfaction and the respect of colleagues. The other thing to remember is that everyone knows what is going on – there are few secrets in organisations. So if I am not getting on well, I know it – and I know you know it too. It is like waiting for the sword of Damocles to fall.
>
> What to do about it?

Start by acknowledging the truth to yourself – 'face the brutal facts', as Jim Collins says in his book *Good to Great*. Take a good hard look at what is happening with the person in your team. Consider what work they do well and the areas in which they are falling down.

Have a conversation to find out how they think they are getting on, including how they are doing on a personal level – domestic upheaval impacts on work effectiveness. If you have tracked their work and spoken honestly in one-to-one meetings, there will be few surprises for you or for them. Make clear that change must occur, and find out what help they need to go forward. Book one-to-ones more frequently, and agree regular milestones along the way.

If this is the first time you have spoken honestly about the problems, expect some distress – you have broken the false sense of security. Explain clearly what the problem is and discuss how they should now act/behave. Set goals, milestones and regular follow-up meetings.

Make it clear that you will do all you can to support them in changing, but resist the temptation to establish another false sense of security. Change comes from a feeling of urgency – honest feedback may be just the thing to concentrate the mind on improving performance or identifying a more appropriate role.

Look back at the section on 'harmlessness' in Chapter 5. This will help you to clarify what is the right action and stick to it.

The concept of 'right person, right job' begs the question as to whether there is a wrong person. Inevitably, some people will not respond to the positive trust and respect offered to them by a great company, and then the appropriate action must be taken. To pretend all is well in the face of evidence to the contrary is bad for the business and the culture.

However it is also true that most people will respond positively to a nurturing environment, and it is the task of managers to make sure that people are working in the job that does justice to their talent, skill set and personality. Great companies will try all the actions outlined above and then look to other areas of the business that might suit a person better. Jo at Flight Centre sees it as part of her role as area manager to match a person to their best job:

> If they are right for the company, we have the job for them somewhere. It's a matter of finding it. I have moved people through a number of possibilities, but mostly we get there in the end.

When you eventually find the right job, the potential that was being limited by the wrong challenge begins to emerge. It is a wonderful experience to see a person thrive – and part of what makes the management task so satisfying.

Teamwork

Managers lead teams, and teams are groups of people who work together to achieve a common purpose. If the task is to be completed, the manager has an important role to play. It is the same message: do not underestimate your significance.

The first step is to get the right people working together. No one is 'wrong' in themselves, but the combination may be. A team full of ideas people who love to brainstorm but fail to put anything into practice is a mistake – they will have fun, but be counter-productive. Equally, a team of implementers can go off down the wrong track out of a desire to get things done and ticked off the 'to do' list.

Take time to consider the skills you need to ensure that the task is completed effectively. If you have to achieve this with a ready-made team, consider the personalities involved. How well do they work together? Are they co-operative people or loners? How effective are their communication skills? Do you know enough about their talents and skills? If not, speak to other people who have worked with them in the past and ask their opinion, access any available psychometric information or talk with the HR department about having an assessment done. All this takes time but will help you make the most of the skills you have, and effectively address the shortfall.

If you can build a new team specifically for the task at hand, look around the business to see if there are high-potential people who would value the challenge. Follow the process above to ensure that you are getting the right people, and do not forget to take the time to talk about the project to see if they are enthusiastic and excited at the prospect. It is also helpful to see how people relate to each other. Emotional intelligence is vital to good teamwork, and it is sometimes better to work with a team who have high EQ and less than ideal skill than to put together the perfect skill profile in a group of people who do not get on.

How do I deal with an existing team that has problems working together?

There are two elements to this:

- picking up an existing team with difficulties
- having difficulties with your own team.

Either way, address the issues so the team can return to effective working.

New team leader:

- If you are an effective listener, talk to people and find out what is happening. Include internal customers and colleagues from other teams.
- Talk with the HR department or a colleague who is known to be a good people person. Use them as a sounding-board for ideas on how to move forward.
- Depending on your people skill, take the next step alone or ask your HR department to provide an internal or external facilitator. If you need to be directly involved in the conversation, definitely use a facilitator.
- Have a meeting/event for the team that identifies what works well and what needs to change. Make an action plan together, including regular milestones and clear measures of success.
- Carry on listening and questioning, in any team of people working together, issues will arise that must be addressed and the sooner the better.
- Appreciate the effort made by everyone.

Existing team leader:

- If the team is malfunctioning, first accept that you are part of the problem. This means that you will be unable to facilitate change yourself, so ask your HR department for help.
- Make clear to the team that you want to hear what they have to say and that you will not hold it against them – and make sure that you don't.
- Ask the facilitator to meet each person in the team separately. It is vital that everyone is heard.
- Listen to the feedback, staying open to what is said, however tough. You will model the openness that is essential for change, and it will be less painful than doing nothing.
- Develop a plan of action with clear measures and support systems.
- Remain as positive as you can. If it is tough, make sure you have

someone to talk to outside the team as a support. Remember: this is the way forward, and feedback – even when hard to hear – is the way to positive change.

- Get support for continuation of the initiative. Use coaching, facilitation, team development and time together to build on the work you have done.

Possible traps

- 'It is just one person causing the problem.' In a team, everyone has responsibility. If one person is hard to deal with, you all have to address the issue. Give straight feedback. Not speaking out is colluding with the problem.
- 'It's the people mix,' meaning evident differences in cultural background, age, education, or whatever else. This can be a cop-out from dealing with the real problem. Be honest with yourself and deal with the underlying issues – see above.
- 'It really is the people mix'. If the mix really does not work, you have to act. Everyone wants to do a good job, so find the right place for them. Identify the true skills and consider where they can best serve the company. If there are relationship issues, give honest feedback before individuals move on, and inform the new team leader so that they can be ready to handle the situation well.
- If you believe you can move your problems to another team, you do yourself no favours. The lack of trust on all sides will cost you. Deal with the issue and you will become known for your courage and effectiveness.

Once you have the right combination of people, you can identify how you want to work together. Proximity to other people with the same objectives means that ideas will flow. At Asda the IT team experimented with moving to sit with the teams they served. It was a great idea and certainly worth a try, but in due course they realised they were losing their identity as an IT team. Now they have returned to their own area, making regular visits to their internal customers. Each morning they go into a 'huddle' where they talk through the IT issues facing them and celebrate the successes of yesterday before going to see their customers. This way the team thrives and maintains its place in the greater team of Asda.

Team identity supports individuals, especially in large companies that can so easily be isolating. It can also lend an extra little something to friendly competition within the company, driving people to greater effort and success for the sake of the team. The team leader sets the tone and ensures that it remains a healthy place, aligned with the principles, while accessing every bit of potential for the good of both team and company.

Remember to celebrate success. Teams work hard to achieve, so encourage them to keep going by appreciating all they give. It is also a wonderful way to build camaraderie – which will in turn improve the teamwork.

The role of hierarchy

In a traditional setting, management functions as part of the hierarchy. You are a manager because you have more seniority, you are more experienced and able than others. In a great company environment, the assumptions are different – you are a manager because you are effective at enabling people to do a good job. That may mean you are more experienced than them, but it certainly does not mean that you are better or more important. Tony DeNunzio, CEO of Asda, claims that you need to break down any hierarchical barriers that exist in the company: remove executive parking places, dining rooms and private offices.

> You'll never create the ultimate culture if you retain symbols of seniority, class and status. At Asda we do have a private plane, but it's for anyone to use when they need to – they just have to book it.

This is a tough one. Lots of people love the trappings of seniority and it can be hard to persuade them to give it up. It is all about status and validation, and how the role gives you a feeling of authority and power. It feels good to have that outward recognition of worth, and you may not want to give it up. It is a decision that only you can make.

However, serving others also brings gains that can be just as gratifying, if not more so. Being part of a highly effective team is a great feeling and produces rewards through excellent business results. In a truly flat structure where effort, commitment and success are valued, you will be lauded for your actual worth, which is considerably more satisfying.

What to do?

Experiment with working as a team member, rather than as the manager, and see what happens:

- Consider how approachable you are. If you work in an office, make sure your door is open and actively invite people in. Go to others and have a chat. Invite people to have lunch with you in the staff room or canteen. Use every opportunity to build a relationship that includes discussing life outside work.
- If you are in a job that carries perks and trappings, experiment with giving them up for a while. If you have a separate dining room at your level, go for lunch today with everyone else and have a chat to someone you do not know.
- Alternatively, take one of your people to lunch with you in the special dining room – trappings make useful treats if you share them.
- Spend today thinking of yourself as serving the team and notice what difference it makes to your behaviour and their responses. Seeing yourself as equal is the first step.

Being a people manager is a great job when it fits you. Experiment with putting others before you, seeking out their potential and delighting in their success. You may find that getting your head up from the piles of work on your desk is the making of the team and the answer to work overload. When you are alone, life is not much fun. Be one of the team and work will start to look up.

As Tony DeNunzio also said 'Take the power of people and make them extraordinary' – that is what your job is about.

Summary

- Great bosses have great people because they set out to serve those who work for them. Make time to get to know those who work for you, their talents, aspirations and skills. Only then can you ensure that they are doing their best job, benefiting you and the business.
- To people who work for you, you are really important. This means how you speak and react is also important. Do not forget it or you will make some big mistakes that lose you trust and respect.
- Mistakes are a useful means of learning. Begin from the stance that no one makes a mistake on purpose and you will help a person learn

and avoid the same mistake in the future. Punish, and they will give up trying.

- Look for the right job for each person. The person who struggles in one job could be a absolute star in another. You may not have the wrong person: it may just be the wrong job. Your task is to support them in finding their true place.
- Tell the truth. Everyone knows when things are not right, so you lose credibility if you back away. And people resent having to pick up the shortfall for persistently under-performing colleagues.
- Celebrate every success, even small ones. It need only be a 'Thank you' or 'Well done', but it will always be appreciated. Give your time and encourage the team to have fun together – it will benefit the work and effectiveness overall.

Stretching potential

As a manager you have a responsibility to hone the talent that comes your way. Be the 'grit in their oyster' and develop the pearl. It will enhance your reputation and further the work of your team, while building the capability of the company.

Thirteen years ago, Roisín took a vacation job on the Asda checkouts. Thanks to their constant search for talent, she now reports to the HR director and is facing her next challenge. She was not at all sure that this was what she wanted, but she agreed to try the graduate scheme for six months. Through careful nurturing and attention to her interest levels, she has been stretched and developed to fulfil the potential that was clearly there.

A wonderful part of the great manager task is to be the grit in the oyster by challenging the comfort zone. High-potential people will not stay in the same role forever. They want to push the boundaries and discover just how much they can achieve. Ignore them and they will go to competitors to improve their CV. Keep the challenge coming and they will stay and move through the organisation.

Roisín never had time to get bored. Every year to 15 months she was given a new challenge. Not only was it exciting, she began to see that she could make a difference – and this is a real turn-on for talented people. She trusted those who managed her, understanding that they would serve both her and the business. So even when the next step was not totally to her liking she recognised it had positive intent.

> This approach is not without its hazards. Sometimes aspiration outweighs potential and a person just cannot reach the required standard. Asda believe it is their fault if they place someone in a job they cannot do. If work is assessed regularly, this is unlikely to happen, but it is always a risk. Then the person has to be re-aligned to their own personal level of excellence. To ease the transition, they may be put on to a separate project before returning to the right job, but it does not always work and people do leave.
>
> It takes a big-hearted person to develop another. Success can mean watching your subordinate pass you by, encouraging others to take on tasks that would otherwise make you shine. However, take on people better than yourself and your work will thrive. Become known as a top talent spotter and everyone will want to work with you.

Action steps

- Think about every person who reports to you. What talents do they have? Let your mind go wide on this, without limiting to the present skill set.
- Who are your high-potential people? How seriously do you take this responsibility? Where do you consider these people could go to in the next five years? Talk with your HR representative or boss about their capabilities.
- Use your network in the company to find out what challenges are on the horizon that might stretch them.
- Be on the lookout for talent in other departments that might be equally challenged by a stint with you.
- Align all this to the business need. Clarify when you can most easily let a person move on without putting too great a strain on the work, yourself, or others in the team.

Hierarchy Honda-style

Honda has always been considered a maverick company in Japan. The company has trouble recruiting the skills it needs and so has become expert at developing talent in-house. And this includes 30 colleagues who are dedicated people managers, honing the talent and skill of managing people.

Management is a skill in its own right. Specific skills can be picked up along the way as managers move around the company. Pauline Wiseman, the present head of HR, previously ran the Honda Institute and prior to that was head of finance – a job she actually arrived prepared for. Her job is to manage people who have the required skill. She just has to create space for them to do the work.

When you have an expert team, the manager does not need to know everything about the task at hand. This is the exact opposite of many companies in which the boss has done the job before you, and so knows at least as much as you do. As many of you reading this book will know, this can be a real drawback. The temptation to become totally absorbed in minutiae is so high that managers can be a real interference in the development of their people.

When Chris Rogers was made corporate PR manager at Honda, he was taken to his desk and left to get on with it. No one showed him the ropes; he had to work it out for himself. So he followed the Three Realities:

- Go to the place.
- Know the actual situation.
- Be realistic.

In other words, get in amongst it to understand where you are and what is important, and then involve the people in moving forward. When Chris has problems he looks to Honda philosophy and wonders what Mr Honda would have done. This company exists through excited, enthusiastic people, and it is managers who enable them to move forward. Without these expert people managers supporting an environment of excellence, you would not be driving your snazzy new Accord.

Action steps

Next time you face a challenge, try the Three Reality principle:

- Go to the place – do not try to work it out from a distance. If your team has a problem, make sure you are where it is occurring.

- Know the actual situation – do not rush into action. Pay attention to what is happening and see what the obstacles are. The most important job may be to remove these, rather than to take action.
- Be realistic – using the information gained from being at the place and knowing the actual situation, be realistic in your assessment and judgement.

Facing the tough decisions

Running a business means facing problems: no one is exempt. And because all problems involve people at some level, it is how you behave that makes the difference.

Ironically, those companies where the guiding principles do not relate to people are most likely to put tough decisions on the back burner. Poor performers are left to languish in a non-job or carried by the team. Everyone knows what is happening, and respect for the management drops a little for each day it continues. The implicit message is that you can get away with murder, so the level of excellence drops down to 'good enough'. If people are not the most important asset, you can talk yourself into being far too busy to deal with the problem.

Great company managers are not allowed that 'luxury' – company principles demand they treat every person with respect. Mick Kent claims that

There are two decisions when dealing with people: first, what is right for the organisational principles, objectives and goals. This is the prime decision. If you have tried everything to bring a person up to standard, but it has failed, then you have to exit them.

Then you are on to number two. Treat that individual in the best way you can – as you would expect to be treated. Don't mix these two things up. Bend over backwards to be as generous and humane as possible – so that person walks out with their head held high and they maintain their dignity as an individual.

Mick is very conscious of removing blocks to high performance – a major part of the job when managing people. Keeping someone in the wrong job creates a blockage for the team and the company, and so must be attended to if everyone is to remain positive and motivated. When the only way is out, your job is to help that person leave in a way that enables them to take on the next job with as much confidence as possible.

Action steps

If you have an under-performer in your team and you are not address-ing the problem, this story will have struck a chord. It is difficult, but you do no one a service by ignoring the truth. If the right job is not in your company, you have to act for the sake of the business and the indi-vidual.

- Talk with the HR department and begin the process.
- When the time comes, be honest with the person – outline the prob-lems that have led to this. Make sure they fully understand so that they can choose a more appropriate job in the future.
- Say what you have appreciated about their work and presence. Remember: they have to go on to other work – help them see where their talents lie.
- Do all you can to ensure that the best possible package is provided.
- Get support internally from people who have done this before and understand the emotional impact on the manager.

Chapter 7

Recruit for attitude, induct for culture

Recruitment is very much a two-way process in a great company. 'Get to know us and see if you really want the job' is just as important as discovering if the prospective colleague suits the business need.

I asked Jack Lowe how they find people who will work well at TD Industries.

> Most people will. No one likes working in a coercive leadership model – they just don't know what else to do.

This is true of all the great companies: most people would love to work there. Microsoft have so many applicants for each role, they had to find ways of cutting down the workload of sorting and interviewing. As a result, they give plenty of information early on so that people can see when the job does not suit them. And imagine how Flight Centre felt when their applications increased by 200 per cent after being named as third best company to work for in the UK.

It is hard work being so popular – but then you also get the pick of the bunch, so to make the best of the opportunity, an effective system of interviewing is essential.

If you just want 'bums on seats', this chapter will be no use to you at all. But then the 'bum on the seat' may not be either! Recruiting to great company culture is a lot more complex than getting headcount. It is business-critical, supporting and maintaining a culture that gets the best out of people, ensuring bottom-line success and excellent customer service. Looked at in that way, filled seats are the least of it.

What are you looking for?

A great company is looking primarily for a person who fits the culture, will feel at home, and is eager to do a good job. It is seeking a colleague, not just an employee – someone who wants to build a career and contribute to the effectiveness of the business. If work is like an extension of the family, then choosing a new addition is an extremely important task.

First you need to know what sort of person will fit into the family. This requires a clear understanding of the elements of the specific culture, what it demands and what it needs. It is back to the guiding principles: not only must you find a person who is comfortable living to these standards, you must demonstrate the standards from the very first contact.

Step 1: Align essential elements of the culture, the demands of the job vacancy and the long-term needs of the company

All too often, interviewing concentrates on whether the person suits the advertised job. In great company terms this is a very limited viewpoint. Microsoft interview for three jobs down the line – so if I apply for a job as an analyst, they will be thinking of what I might do over the next five years. Only then will they know if I have the potential to suit their needs. Great companies recruit mainly at entry level and develop people in house. 'Growing their own' means that the culture strengthens and all that wonderful experience and the customer relationships stay in house. But they must choose people who have the potential in the first place.

It is also really important to recognise that taking the easy option now simply stores up problems for the future. Dealing with underperformance or lack of team fit will take up far more time and have a greater impact on the work outcome than thorough recruitment.

Step 2: Understand the type of person who fits into the culture

This issue of seeking the right person to fit can be a bit contentious. People become concerned that it may be a recipe for cloning, developing a cult, or putting diversity at risk. Of course it can be all those, if allowed to be – but then that would not really be a great company. Diversity at all levels is what keeps us honest, creative and exciting – and this is what great companies crave.

However, they do need people to fit in with and be comfortable living the guiding principles. It will not work if, like Flight Centre, you believe passionately in equality, to hire someone who loves hierarchy.

It is not fair on them or on other colleagues. Principles are so central to company culture that they must align with the personal principles of the colleagues, or it will be impossible to live them day to day. But honesty, equality, respect and integrity work regardless of gender, ethnicity, sexual preference or religion – they choose anyone!

All too often the HR function is left alone to select new colleagues. Great companies bring managers and teams into the loop, clarifying exactly what type of person will balance the team and provide the best business mix. Taking just anyone can slow the team down and cause more problems than the original lack of staff, so it is important to get it right.

Step 3: Make your advertising clear

There are many ways to advertise for new people. Richer Sounds get a lot of applications via colleagues. Their 'Introduce a friend' scheme pays out £250 if the new person works there for more than six months. On the basis that the applicant will have heard what it is really like to work at Richer from their friend or a family member, there is a strong chance that they will fit in. This is a method used by many of the companies – recommendations are a great way to find those who will enjoy and benefit from the culture.

There is just one element to watch out for here. People tend to have friends who are like them, so be aware of the diversity balance and take action to ensure that it remains healthy.

Another thing Richer Sounds does is place advertisements in their shops and magazines. Because the company is looking for people who are passionate about hi-fi, the company's customers are a good source of colleagues. Flight Centre advertises where young travellers are most likely to look, and Timpsons place notices in the shops to tempt enthusiastic customers to apply. It is making the best of your attributes – using a positive customer experience also to find the right people to fit the work.

Step 4: Find out all you can at interview – identify the attitude and style of the candidate early on, to give you and the candidate the best chance that they will stay

Often this is the preserve of recruitment agencies – to find a clutch of possible candidates, and do the initial testing, so cutting down the workload. This is highly effective when the principles that guide the recruitment agency match those of the company. If they do not, the process will cost time and money, not save it. Great recruiters strive to understand the company culture and get alongside the managers concerned to ensure that they are matching not just to job but to attitude. Then they are worth their weight in gold.

TD Industries, like many of the other companies, put applicants through a whole battery of tests – attitude, intelligence, and so forth. This is one way of gaining information without the risk of seeing only 'best behaviour'. Putting on the right face for the duration of an interview is possible; day after day in the midst of hard work it is much more difficult.

But nothing compares to personal contact. It is common for the interviewing process to take some time, with each prospective colleague meeting a variety of people. Richer Sounds bring in their senior store colleagues to talk with interviewees – 'We are looking for friendly, outgoing, likeminded people, regardless of their knowledge of hi-fi.' This can be evaluated through conversation in which store managers will be the best judges of how candidates would relate to customers.

It does not always work. As Jack Lowe says:

> We spend hours with people and follow up references, but we do get fooled. Often people select themselves out – if they think we are nuts. They don't have to be out of the same cookie cutter, they just need to fit our principles.

Most losses occur in the first six months. If people stay longer than that, they are generally there to stay for the long term.

Step 5: Give the team a say – let them work together as part of the interview process to see if it is the right mix

This serves in three ways.

- It enables the team to get a sense of the prospective colleague and whether they will fit in workwise and socially.
- It ensures that the applicant has a clear idea of the actual work and is not looking through rose-tinted glasses. They have a clear picture of what the job involves before finally making a decision.
- You get to see if they are really aligned to the working principles.

When the team have met the new person and worked with them, it is important to ask their opinion. This is a good way of ensuring that you get the right person in the right job, and it is an opportunity to show respect for colleagues. It is important to be clear how you will use their feedback.

At Flight Centre you cannot say no 'because you don't like their hair band'. In other words, if you want to reject someone, you must have a very good reason. But if that reason is there, they will listen and not put the person into the team. However, this does not mean that they will turn the person away from the company. Having got that far, it is likely that they will fit into Flight Centre somewhere – it is just a matter of finding the right job. Once that happens, even the most sluggish person can fly.

'Surely the most important thing is to find people who can do the job? If they want the work, they'll make the effort to fit in.'
You are probably right, but do you want a person who must work at fitting into the environment rather than getting on with the job? Most companies do put most emphasis on skill – it is a natural reaction to concentrate on the most pressing need. However, it will trip you up in the long run. People at work only for the job, who feel at odds with the culture, will not stay – and then you are back to where you started, wasting money on additional recruitment.

If you need a high level of skill, you must recruit for that, but not in isolation. Be conscious of how the person will fit in and what you see as their potential. Remember that if you can choose someone now who can develop a career in-house, you will retain all the company and client knowledge they build up over time, keeping information and skill in the company instead of sending it to your competitors.

Action steps
The first step is to gain clarity about the people who fit best in your team – ie those who will work together well to give the best results. To make sure you understand, ask yourself and team members the following questions:

- What is the team like when everyone is working to their optimum? Be specific about the characteristics – ie friendly, supportive, challenging, exciting, etc.
- What is the characteristic in the team that allows that culture to develop? For example, it might be that the team is supportive because they pay attention to each other and listen to what

people say. Having realised what make the team click you will know what characteristics you are looking for in a new recruit; for example, if you have a lively, extrovert team you won't want someone who like to work alone in peace and quiet.

- What are the difficult aspects of the team tasks? Identify the personalities that are best suited to handling them. For example, if the job requires handling frustrated customers, choosing a highly outspoken person will be of little value – but if the job might involve challenging assumptions from other parts of the business, an outspoken person might be just right.

When you have the feedback, analyse it and build a picture of the person best suited to maximise the positives and handle the difficulties. This will also give you useful information about the present team that will support team development. Talk with your HR department about ways to build on the information gathered.

Once you have a clear picture of the type of person you need, talk with your HR representative or manager to make sure that the present recruitment process will suit your needs:

- How effective has it been to date? Take into account your retention rate and the fit of people in your team at present.
- Look at the tests that are included to ensure that they give you the information you need about character as well as about skills.
- Look at the information given about the company and the team. Make sure that applicants have a clear understanding of the working environment. Telling the absolute truth from the outset will reduce the risk of mistakes. Some companies bring the chosen candidate in for a day or half-day so that he or she can choose from sound knowledge. See if this would work for you.
- Review where you advertise and make sure that you are reaching the right audience.

The induction process

Principles underpin the way an organisation works. Sometimes they are spoken directly, sometimes they are implicit and newcomers learn in short order 'how we do things round here'. The formal and informal induction period ensures that newcomers learn how to relate to senior leaders, who the main influencers are, who they need to be careful of, how long they need to work each day, and whether it is acceptable to have a laugh and for how long. The list is endless, but integral to each and every group of people who spend time together.

Most organisations provide a written version of principles as part of the induction package, since it is so basic to the smooth running of the business. What is not always clear is whether this written list describes the actual principles that determine the environment or whether it is really a list of aspirations, while quite different principles reign supreme.

Principles are evoked by the heart and let us know what is acceptable, so we can sleep well at night. You can tell people how to behave and it will have some effect, but you will only have them truly onside when you connect at heart level.

This is where stories come in. The tales of life in your company will help people understand what is really important and why. Inviting long-term colleagues to induction sessions to tell their stories will do more to build a sense of belonging and understanding than any presentation. On his last visit to the UK, Mr Honda turned down a grand programme of events, preferring to shake hands with everyone who worked for him. How powerful is that, compared to the bald words that 'Honda places great importance on the individual'?

Induction is the chance to instil company principles and the behaviour that underpins them. People then know 'how we do things round here', how to approach problems and mistakes, and what to expect from success. If a good induction programme is one that leaves people inspired about work, can you afford it to be delayed or not to be the best use of time?

Talk with the newest recruits in your team and find out how useful the induction process was to them:

• Did they go on the course soon enough?

• How well did it prepare them for life in the company?
• Did your behaviour match what they were led to expect?
• What would they like to have known; what would they tell newcomers from their work experience?

Give this feedback to the people responsible for induction. Do this in a way that is supportive rather than critical. Have a discussion and share your thinking about what is effective and what might change. Find out how can you support them in making it more effective.

Consider what you can offer alongside the formal process:

- At a team meeting talk about the team culture and what people need to know when they join. If you encourage people to be honest, this will be a really interesting conversation that will also bring the team together in a new way.
- Make a list of the 'things we do round here', both serious and fun – eg who makes the coffee in the morning through to how to deal with mistakes and how to approach the senior leaders.
- Talk about how you would like to have been included when you first joined. Encourage everyone to take responsibility for including others.
- Make a plan for your next recruit, remembering that they will be cautious and unsure – find the way to make them feel at home.

- Allocate one person to look after the newcomer for the first week, and encourage that relationship to continue as a sounding-board in times of uncertainty.
- Make a note in the diary for three months ahead to check how it went and if appropriate to make adjustments for the next person.

Consider your own behaviour:

- Make sure your actions match the company/team words.
- Ask for feedback from new recruits – do we do what we say?
- In team meetings, using the original conversation as a base, encourage feedback about behaviour that fits well or does not fit at all – help to keep each other honest.

At Asda, new recruits are put on 100 days of induction, during which time they move around all the different departments in the company. This means that they understand the interconnections between departments, giving them a sound basis for the future. At the end of the process they are invited to lunch with senior leaders in their part of the company. One of the questions asked is 'How well did we do? We told you at the outset about our company principles – are we as good as we said we are?' The answer is generally that they are better, which is heartening. It is really important to stay open to feedback in these areas. The status quo is incredibly tempting – after all, it probably works 'well enough' – a phrase that is the death knell of excellence.

Richer Sounds send people for a three-day training intensive in their own facilities – a converted barn at the back of Julian Richer's home. Not only does this bring them up to scratch with the product, they bond together and begin to feel 'part of the family'. It is a relaxed time: they learn about the work and make best use of the wonderful amenities – pool, cinema, snooker and badminton. Within a month they are taken on a tour of the main offices in London, and if they have not done so already, they meet Julian.

But this is not the end of it at Richer. Throughout these early days, managers are on the lookout for high-potential colleagues, and within three to four months, if they have the ambition, they will be on the management development programme. So induction not only provides colleagues with an excellent start to their new work, it enables the company to highlight their new leaders and pick up the baton as fast as possible.

This leads to a significant element of great companies – that they look to develop their own leaders in-house. Recruitment and induction must always have a eye for succession. Think about it. You are not looking for your new CEO when she is ready to take the job – you are trying to spot her when she is new and unformed in leadership terms.

It creates a dual pressure:

- The first is to keep a flow of high-potential people interested in the company early in their careers. Because you are a great company this is really important, and as long as you are known to be a great company it is unlikely to be a problem. Good people want to make the best of themselves, and so will seek out great cultures.
- Taking people primarily at entry level can lead to a lack of stimulation higher up the organisation. Looking for ways to inspire and excite people to develop and keep challenging is a vital weapon against atrophy. TD Industries got stuck about 15 years ago, and so had to seek out ways of stimulating creativity through outside contacts with the community.

All of which shows the need to keep honest and conscious about what is happening. A great company is only as great as the people involved, and if they become complacent, the culture is in danger. Some companies will address this by bringing in an external leader to shake it all up, but this may cost the culture. A strong 'command-and-control' interim leader will create change in a stuck and unproductive business, but time may then be needed to repair the self-esteem of those who remain.

Staying in touch with a reality once you are in it is really hard – 'You cannot see the picture when you are inside the frame.' Newcomers to the business are a perfect opportunity to look through fresh eyes – see yourselves as others see you and act on the feedback. It will help the culture stay great.

Summary

- Look for attitude first. You must find people who will live the company principles on a daily basis.
- Make sure that possible recruits spend time with their team doing the work to get a real sense of what it will be like.
- Be totally honest about the workplace. It is a waste of time to persuade people and take the time to train them if they are unlikely to stay.
- Look for potential – what job will they do in three years' time?
- Provide a thorough induction that helps newcomers understand the job and the culture.
- Ask them to give you feedback on how well you live the guiding principles. Are you doing what you say you do? Act on their feedback.

Interviewing great-company-style

Recruitment is a major investment – why risk taking on someone who will leave within the first six months so you have to begin all over again? Effective recruitment contributes to high retention, which is good for the budget and the knowledge and experience base in the company.

Jo is an area leader in Flight Centre with responsibility for a number of teams in the London region. When interviewing, she looks for energy and passion, a positive attitude to the work and a spark that leads her to believe the person will fit the fun culture. Together with her colleagues she puts each person through seven to ten days of selection.

Sonal went through the process and confirms how tough it is, but each step conveyed a little more about the company and encouraged her to keep going. The final stage was an 'in-store assessment day' (ISA), when she was invited in to spend a day with her would-be team. She sat alongside her future colleagues, seeing what the job involved, how hard the work was, and learned something of the experience of working with the public. Jo looked for how she interacted with the team, watched how much she enjoyed herself, and tried to gauge whether Sonal could maintain her energy level. She wanted to be sure that Sonal really wanted the job, so she answered each question really honestly, never once pulling her punches. 'We have to recruit the right people, and we will only do that if we are totally honest.'

Work at FC can sound really appealing when you hear about the buzz nights, awards, cheap travel and great bonuses. So it is vital that applicants get a taste of the tough day-to-day work. By 5 pm, Sonal had got the message. In fact, she was totally convinced she wanted the job. The team were equally positive, and she is now coming to the end of her first year.

At the outset, Jo herself was less sure and left FC after her first nine months in the job. She worked in similar companies and undertook some travel of her own. Eventually, the penny dropped and she realised she would rather be at FC. She called 'Boxer' (Gary Hogan, MD) direct and asked if there was a job for her. 'I thought you'd never ask,' was his immediate reply, reflecting his determination never to close the door on a good employee.

The detailed results delivered at the end of each week provide a record of performance, so it is easy to see how well a person worked in the past. The company will not take back an ex-colleague who had difficulty with the job, but someone who succeeded and enjoyed the pace is welcomed back with open arms.

Action steps

Remember: you are not just filling a position, you are building the future of your company. Mistakes made now impact on succession plans, never mind seeing those you train and nurture walk out of the door.

- Check out your record to date. How effective are you in finding a) the right people for the job, and b) people you can develop?
- For your next recruit, consider what you need for this job and the future. Identify what your needs will be in three years: what talent must you train now to fill that gap? Interview with this in mind.
- How much information do you give applicants about the company? Ask new colleagues what else they would like to have been told about the job.

- Include members of the relevant team in the selection process. Talk with them about what they believe the team needs and ask how they will spot it. Make sure that those who will be with the new person day to day feel involved.
- Seek feedback from new colleagues, their colleagues and their boss. What could have been done better? How might the process be improved?

Interviewing from a principles base: getting the right people on board

If you want to maintain a great culture, employ people who will live the company principles. This begins with the initial interview, giving people an experience of how the company works, allowing them to assess whether they can work happily in this environment, and starting the process of alignment.

The message about principles has to be consistent and on-going, beginning at first contact. Even at interview, prospective colleagues must be in no doubt about what is important. If they believe in different things, better to find out now than deal with the consequences at a later stage. Companies have a variety of ways of getting the message across, but it is always a rigorous process to separate the serious from the sightseers.

You must really want a job at St Luke's Advertising Agency – the interview process is definitely not for the faint-hearted. One shareholder (colleague) was drawn to the informality that came across from the website, so she contacted them direct. Although no job was available at the time, they invited her to visit. She went for an informal interview that was to become the first of many, meeting in all 12 different people for individual conversations. Topics ranged from work and hobbies to what risk she is most proud to have taken. It seems that this was the clincher. On holiday in Spain she and her friends cycled around a tight bend and spotted a young man standing on the side of a cliff. Within seconds, to their horror, he had jumped. She approached the edge, fearing the worst, only to see him a very long way down in a deep lagoon. Imagine her trepidation when he waved and called her to join him. So to her proudest moment. Stripping off to her bikini, she too jumped over the edge and 'flew' down to the inviting blue water. This was apparently a good metaphor for life in St Luke's, and she got the next available job.

It is true that St Luke's loses people who are offered good jobs in the meantime – not everyone is willing to wait – and this does have a cost. On the other hand, life at St Luke's is informal with few traditional boundaries to hang on to, and it is important to give the flavour of this from the outset. People who last the distance will have as good an idea as it is possible to get of what life will be like.

Other great companies go through their own version of this process. Getting the right people is paramount – attitude before skill is a common theme – 'We can upskill them later, as long as they are the right people.' The right people will take on new challenges, move into new areas and keep ideas and suggestions flowing. In essence, they keep the company alive – and great.

Action steps

- Consider the actual culture of the workplace and identify the people who work there most effectively. What is it that means they suit the culture? Specify the attributes, talents and personality traits they bring. Check your interview questions to see if they help you identify people with these characteristics.
- Revisit the interview process. Do you rush forward in order to get a 'bum on the seat'? How well is this working? How might you make the process more rigorous and effective?
- Find out when most people leave – this will give you an idea of how successful you really are. If you have a high number of leavers in the first year, you have not given them a clear enough picture of what to expect.
- Revisit the exit interviews of those who have left. If possible, contact some of them to find out what would have encouraged them to stay. Find out what would have given them a better sense of the workplace and helped them settle better at the outset.
- Talk with your team/section: share ideas about how to describe and demonstrate the culture. Arrange for them to meet applicants for a chat.
- Great companies are very honest at interview. Ask a colleague/friend outside the business to read through the information given and describe what this leads them to expect. Talk with new recruits to find out if what you said is what they got.

Interviewing and induction at Microsoft

Once you are known for a great company culture, applications will increase. In order to save time and ensure that you find the pick of the bunch, a thorough process is imperative.

When the technology market was buoyant, Microsoft needed to take in large numbers of people to deliver the needs of their customers. Their recruitment requirement is less these days, but applications still flood through the door because people know that it is a fantastic place to work and develop a career. Separating the high-flyers from the rest is a constant job, and Susie has recently worked out a new procedure with her team in HR.

The first point of call is the website where applicants can look for specific jobs. To encourage self selection, job specifications are accompanied by pen pictures describing what doing the job will really be like. Having joined only 18 months ago, Susie remembers how hard it was to settle in. The culture is one of working hard, playing hard and being very autonomous. Changes occur at great speed. People who like certainty in their working lives will know straight away that this is not the place for them.

Microsoft has found a recruitment partner that works to similar principles. When an application arrives on the website, the recruiters respond with a phonecall to test the water which, if promising, is followed by a first interview with them at Microsoft offices in Thames Valley Park. Until recently this was always held in the atrium – a place buzzing with life, where colleagues have coffee, hold meetings, talk on the phone. It gives a real feel of the flexible style and excitement of the work, but has also unnerved some applicants who were afraid they would be distracted. Now people are given the choice to meet in an office if they prefer.

A CV is then sent to the hiring manager and the HR department for them to consider on a competency basis, and if all is well the applicant is called back for a second interview where he or she attends an assessment day. This includes competency evaluation and role plays involving prospective peers, plus meetings with HR and the relevant managers. The final stage is a third visit to meet a senior leader/stakeholder for the stamp of approval.

Once an offer is made and accepted, the new hire is invited in to meet the team they will work with. Because Susie had a long wait as she worked out her notice, she attended their Christmas party, and so had a good chance to find out all about her new colleagues.

Induction
The first morning is a late start to ease the entry, so at 11 am new colleagues gather for a coffee and an introduction to the logistics of working at MS. Each person is given a buddy to look out for them in the early days, and together they go for lunch with the managers. In the afternoon they have a tour of the building, sort out their desk, computer, phones, etc, and go home at 4 pm.

Managers do the local induction, and three weeks later all new starters in the UK are called together for an afternoon meeting. They play a game along the lines of *Monopoly*, which builds their knowledge of the company overall. Their task

is to build a business selling MS products. They get points for spotting significant people along the way, recognising the guiding principles when they meet them, and being able to identify different elements of the software that will help them sell their wares. The winners are those with the most successful business at the end of the afternoon.

The final cherry on the cake is a visit to Seattle – Induction 101. All the global new starters meet together at the headquarters to learn about the worldwide company – a great treat that is highly informative, and a chance to begin building that all-important network.

The end result is a 3 per cent staff turnover rate. And when people do leave it is generally in order to do something entirely different, like study homeopathy or train as a pilot!

Action steps

- If you work with a recruitment agency, how closely aligned are you on guiding principles? Ensuring that you are will ease the selection process.
- Make sure that the agency really knows the role involved. Get agency people in to talk with managers and individuals who do the job, so that they can give a clear description to potential recruits.
- Do you enable people to get a good feel of the working atmosphere? Think about the elements that make work in your organisation/team distinctive and make sure that people get a feel of this at the outset. If it does not suit them, they can then choose to opt out.

- Do all the stakeholders get a chance to meet prospective colleagues? Remember: if this place has a feel of commitment and family, significant people need to be involved.
- Induction must be delivered immediately to be of real benefit. In some companies it takes place months later – this will add some value, but in an entirely different way. Ensure that you provide the best local and company induction you can in the first days. Do this in a way that is aligned to the culture. If you work in a fun, exciting workplace, therefore, make the induction fun and exciting.
- If your company is global or nationwide, consider bringing all the new people together. This will enable them to get a sense of the full entity, to see where their work fits into the whole, and to begin building a company-wide network that will stand them in good stead.

Chapter 8

Taking responsibility

Great companies are hothouses for people development. That is why head-hunters are on the phone as soon as a company is named 'great'. If you can manage to recruit someone from a great company, you know you will have quality. Giving people responsibility and supporting them as they learn is the best way to hone talent. Challenge brings out the best in the best.

Bromford Housing Group applied to get on the list as a benchmarking opportunity. They wanted to know how they were doing in relation to the best. Imagine their surprise when they came in at number 5. Let's be clear, this is not a grand place with gyms, crèche or concierge services. In fact, to quote Nick, Housing Services director, 'We are not into flash offices and we have strains on accommodation in our area offices – we are definitely still on a journey there.' It must be their strategy of people development that is earning them the accolade.

> We hadn't quite appreciated the importance of teamwork, sense of purpose, standing for the principles, supporting each other and personal development opportunities. They clearly matter far more than we realised. The *Sunday Times* endorses that we have been doing the right thing. There are many other things we need to do to stay up with the market – but we seem to have the foundation right.

This demonstrates clearly that giving responsibility and providing the necessary support is more important than all the lovely perks wealthy companies can provide. These are fantastic and no one in their right mind would refuse them, but this is not all it takes to make a great company. Providing the chance to grow and develop is so appealing that people will choose it over anything else.

Why is responsibility so important?

There are three reasons.

First, being enabled, encouraged and expected to take full responsibility for a piece of work shows respect. It is recognition that you are an able person in your field and there is no reason why you should not do the very best job. Giving people space to achieve and the support to do so, without watching like a hawk, is grown-up behaviour that evokes a grown-up response.

Second, it is a wonderful way to develop skill and ability. Doing the same job over and over is the fastest way to brain death. If you are stretched to grapple with a problem or challenge, you will also be alert to ideas and suggestions for your own or other areas of the business.

Third, when people take responsibility, it becomes their company, not just somewhere they go each day from 9 to 5. This is the perfect antidote to the dreaded discussions about 'them' who are commonly believed to be the cause of every upset. In a great company, blaming senior leaders or managers is not an option. A responsible person is expected to do something about it when they encounter a problem – look at their contribution, talk to the person concerned or take appropriate action. This is what 'empowered' means, when each person takes on their part of the whole, addressing issues as they arise and looking for the best way forward. It has a lot to do with that wonderful sparkle in the eyes of great company colleagues – 'Through tough times and fun times, we are in this together.' Now *that's* exhilarating!

From all perspectives, individual and organisation are winners. The old pattern of sticking to the same job over a long time belongs in the dim and distant past. A job for life is out of the window, so a career has to be built in a different way. These days it is all about being employable. The company that wants people to be fully involved provides interesting challenge, an opportunity that is very attractive to 'high-potentials'. And 'high-potentials' who want to extend their reach are very attractive to strong companies. It is a marriage made in heaven.

There are many companies out there who provide challenge, but without great company culture to support it. Colleagues are stretched, which benefits the CV, but all too often there is a cost in pressure and overload. When principles favour money rather than people, there is little tracking of the human cost. People have to take care of themselves, so they get what they can out of the company and take off to pastures new when the strain gets too much. We have all heard of organisations that when named on the CV open any door you may wish. But we have also heard that working there is a complete nightmare that can be managed only for so long. Successful they may be, but caring they certainly are not, and the recruitment bills are astronomical.

As the support/challenge quadrant demonstrates (see Table 3), getting the balance right is paramount. Too much support and not enough challenge will develop complacency – when there is little expectation, some will coast and others will leave. Equally, too much demand with little support will create high stress levels, prompting people to leave for better workplaces when their energy runs out. Too little all round leads to apathy and only those who do not care or have low self-esteem will remain. Provide support and challenge in equal balance and you will hold the best people and get the best out of them.

TABLE 3   ORGANISATIONAL INVOLVEMENT: SUPPORT/CHALLENGE

	Low support	High support
High challenge	HIGH STRESS When challenge is high and support is low, people live up to demands but there is a very real cost to their health and commitment. They will go on for as long as they can, then leave or burn out.	GREAT COMPANIES Challenge is high, matched by equally high levels of support. This enables people to stretch into their full potential, knowing that they can ask for help when they need it, and be respected for doing so.
Low challenge	APATHY Low support and low challenge is the ideal environment if you want to amble through life, but dreadful for those who want to do a good job. When few demands are made and there is little support to achieve, good people leave, if they don't lose their self-esteem first.	COMPLACENCY Plenty of support is the recipe for a great time. When there is little challenge to balance it, people start to coast through the working day. High-potential people lose interest and go to places that will stretch them more effectively.

Personal development in a great company culture

Personal development is central to the business in a great company, and so is handled more carefully than in the high-stress cultures described above. The pressures are the same and the need to push forward is equally important. However, the level of care, appreciation and encouragement in the tough times is entirely different.

Everyone is seen as having potential that can be developed, and the stories are countless of people coming in as temps to sort out the filing and ending up in a significant role in the company. Talent can easily be hidden, so great companies seek it out. Regardless of age, gender, race or creed, if you are interested, proactive and come up with ideas for moving forward, you will be supported in doing so.

Opportunities for taking an informal leadership role are numerous when people care about the company and cherish its success. Being aware that something could work better and not acting on it is unacceptable in a culture of commitment and responsibility. It may be the senior leader or the cook who comes up with the bright idea to improve the running of the day, and it will be equally well received from either.

Colleague circles in each Asda store are designed to maximise on just that awareness. Service is for a rotation of two years and volunteers have to apply to the incumbent circle, making a presentation demonstrating their attributes for the job. It is an interesting approach: each person gets experience in presenting to a group and also has to own up to what they do well – an oft-neglected subject in the UK. The circle is given an agenda the company requires them to attend to, and the circle itself raises the issues it sees as important, coming up with ideas for action. It is a fantastic concept that could so easily stray into a whinging session, bemoaning the fact that 'they' are not doing enough. Persisting with the concept of responsibility, each circle has been given a budget of £5,000 per year to use without reference to the company. So if they think it is important to have daily newspapers for colleagues, it can buy them; if it wants the tiles changed in the toilets, it can get it done. This means that members of the circle can drive change and enjoy ownership of what happens.

'That sounds like an awful lot of money for people to do with as they wish. Not every company can do that – and anyway, it probably wouldn't be used wisely.'

Remember: this is what works for Asda. You must find what works for you.

It is an interesting assumption that people will not use money wisely. Resist the temptation to retreat into a 'parent-child' relationship. As a manager or leader, you will have some level of power over the other – how you choose to use that power is another matter. Because certain decisions are in your gift, it does not mean that the people who report to you are incapable. They are probably adults with rent or a mortgage to pay, kids to raise, families to care for, a car to maintain and holidays to arrange. Why would they lose all that common sense when they come to work?

Problems arise where there is little respect or trust between staff and managers. When people feel taken advantage of, they may try to balance the scales. The answer lies not in withholding but in *giving* respect to the adults you work with, and ensuring that they feel a sense of ownership for the business. If they are really part of the team, there is little chance that they will use money badly. Most of the time, including and trusting people evokes commitment and care of the budgets on all fronts. Many ideas for cutting costs have emerged in just this way, because high-trust cultures attract low costs. It is in low-trust cultures where the costs go through the roof.

Action steps

Begin with your own team:

- On a scale of 1 to 10, how well do you trust the people you work with?
- Identify those you have confidence in and those you are less sure of.
- List your reasons for and against trusting each person.
- Work out what you need to do to build up your trust levels.

Trust is built through a relationship, so the more you understand a person, the clearer you will be about trusting. If you have not already done so:

- Book a time to speak to each person.
- Find out as much as you can about their work experience. Do they have everything required to do the job? Do they feel well

supported? What do they need from you that you do not currently supply? What are their aspirations for the future?
- Give feedback about your own experience of their work – appreciations and concerns.
- Agree actions to address shortfalls for both of you.
- Make a date to check on progress in two weeks, and keep it. Show that you can be trusted and that you are not just doing this because you are reading a book on management.

Once you have spoken with everyone individually:
- Call a team meeting and find out what they want to change in the team environment.
- Having listened to their concerns and ideas, choose something you can hand over fully, including giving an appropriate budget.
- Talk through the project with them, assure them of your support.
- Agree update meetings and take a back seat.
- Intervene only if absolutely necessary – model sticking to your word – ie role model the behaviour you need from them.
- Celebrate success, and if the project is not totally successful, take the learning and celebrate the process.

If you have concerns, be open about them. This is an exercise in trust-building, so do not withhold concern, be honest. Trust does not mean avoiding the tough conversations: it means having them in a respectful and considerate manner.

When to offer development?

'Always' is the quick answer. However, every organisation has a range of people with different needs. Not everyone is a high flyer, and even high flyers go into abeyance, depending on what happens in their lives. A company has to be aware of this and react accordingly. It is also true that anyone can come up with a good idea, so making sure that everyone keeps a mindset of curiosity and interest is important.

Some companies provide a small budget for personal development of any type, like the 'Make yourself more interesting' fund at St Luke's or the funds to go to an evening class of your choice at TD Industries. Jack Lowe Jnr is a firm believer that if a person is thinking and learning in any direction, it affects their ability to learn at work. So taking up an evening class in pottery or ancient history will benefit the company by keeping the brain exploring and inquisitive. The old phrase 'If you don't use it, you'll lose it' holds true for great companies.

Some of the best ideas come from people who work on the front line with customers or the specific product. *No leader or manager, however effective, can have all the answers.* Ensuring that colleagues are alert and interested makes excellent business sense. The last thing you want is people who notice what doesn't work and do nothing about it. Leaving all decisions and concerns to the management is the kiss of death to innovation and high performance. As Mark Davies of Honda is acutely aware: 'People walk in every day seeing things that don't work well. We have to access that knowledge.'

Some colleagues have reached the peak of their ambition, or had little work ambition to begin with. They enjoy doing a good job, seeing their friends, then going home to a quiet evening with the family or a night out with their mates. Work is not the be-all and end-all. They have exciting hobbies, prefer a quiet life or are saving up to go around the world. This does not mean that they stop thinking or coming up with ideas. Intellectual snobbery is a killer to company development. Everyone brings value – it is a wise company that makes the best of it all.

When people have a specific talent or are bright and ambitious, it makes sense to bring them on. Part of a manager's role is to spot potential anywhere in the business and make the most of it. It may be the person with innumerable good ideas who is not afraid to speak out; the one who listens to the good ideas and sets about forming a plan of action; or the person who can see the flaw and finds a creative way of changing course. Equally, it might be the excellent networker who can support and enable a project team exceptionally well.

As manager, the task is to be a talent scout extraordinaire, ever on the lookout for skills and abilities, even when they do not fit neatly into the usual box. To do this job effectively, high self-esteem is essential. It is really hard to foster talent if you feel unsure of your own position. This is a good reason for building a positive relationship with your manager, so you are clear where you stand, and for doing the same with those who report to you. Personal security enables talent, which builds a strong business.

Appraisals

For managers, the usual time to consider development is at the regular appraisal. This is the moment for looking at progress to date, identifying what works well, what needs to change and how best to move forward. In some organisations it is a process that takes place once a year, sometimes in a very rigorous way, sometimes perfunctorily. Great managers make this a positive occasion, providing feedback and options for going forward. For others it is to be dreaded or even avoided – and some managers always 'happen' to be called away at the last minute.

Make appraisals a priority and never put off without rescheduling at the first opportunity. It is really important for both colleague and company. Endless preparation will have been done, assessing work since the last discussion, maybe getting feedback from work colleagues, and ideas for the next stage ... For some it is like preparing for an examination, with all the accompanying stress and anxiety. Put off the date and you divert their energy into anticipation and concern, away from productive activity. Equally, if you disappoint that amount of commitment, it will not happen again – a level of trust will be lost that will take a long time to recover.

Of course, not everyone is so rigorous about their appraisal meeting. Many people do nothing in the hope that it will go away, seeing the meeting as anything from too daunting through to pointless. Only if the manager takes it seriously, demanding that they do too and using it as a meaningful development tool, will they see the true value and begin to get something out of it.

Discuss progress at regular intervals. This may be a formal appraisal or a one-to-one check-in, but it needs to happen. Limit feedback to a thorough review just once a year and you risk missing something, especially with high-potential people. They travel a long way in a year and this needs to be acknowledged and validated. Keeping track is the only way to ensure that they make the most of their chances – the direction may need to change, energy levels for the present challenge may drop, and the sooner it is picked up the better. Some companies like Flight Centre have monthly appraisals to ensure a tight hold on the next steps. Others like Hiscox have a formal appraisal once a year, with a mid-term review and monthly one-to-ones that are sacrosanct. Whatever you call it, check in with your people more rather than less.

Appraisal often determines bonus or salary review. This varies in great companies for a very good reason. People who are growing and developing are sure to make mistakes. According to Mark Davies, 'If you are brave enough to be exposed, you also know you won't win all the time.' Great companies want people to take risks in learning, experimenting and innovating, and no one can do that without periodic mistakes. If salary review is tied to development, you have a conundrum. Who in their right mind will take big risks if it might cost a jump in salary? The temptation will be to play safe.

In Hiscox the performance level indicators are set half for development, which will not affect pay, and half for performance, which will influence salary. At Flight Centre, performance is clearly measured and bonus is given on all work once the 'cost of chair' is covered – ie bring in enough work to cover the cost of having a shop or office for you to work in and you get a bonus on everything else.

Encouraging development without penalising people through pay awards is vital to building potential. However, it is also important to reward success. It is a fine line to travel, but one that needs addressing continuously.

How to develop people

Training is one way forward. External or bespoke in-house programmes address specific issues but run the risk of keeping learning separate from the workplace, tucked away neatly in the smart binder. To make the most of these opportunities the manager must follow up and maybe provide a coach or internal mentor to track action in the weeks and months following.

A method used in great companies is to provide 'real-time' challenge in the workplace by giving people projects that stretch them, or by seconding them to another department for a specific piece of work. This ensures that learning is tied to work, bringing fresh ideas and 'out of the box' thinking. For some, it is taking on a totally different job, even if that means retraining. The latter carries an inevitable cost as the person gets to grips with the new role, but this is balanced by the value of a different approach with all the fresh thinking and creativity that that brings. It depends how you see life: is it better to do the same thing more or to look for new ways of approaching the tried and tested? Individual development fuels company growth and change.

Moving out of the box is the great company way forward. It can be tough and stressful on occasions, so support must be in good supply. David, a young manager from Kent Messenger Group discovered this when the time came to appraise a reluctant and older direct report. She took her concerns to David's manager and was told 'You have two choices. Have your appraisal with David, or don't have one.' That his manager was so convinced it would work encouraged them both, and the appraisal meeting went remarkably well. Facing the unfamiliar is not easy. It needs all those concerned to be willing to do their best. In this case, the senior manager maintained support for David in the face of challenge, David was brave enough to continue, and the direct report was open, honest and generous, learning 'not to take people at face value'.

The value of mistakes

Mistakes are inevitable in a forward-thinking company. Innovators get used to the feeling of getting it wrong and spend time looking to what they have learned from the result. Hearing stories about Edison and the light bulb or J. K. Rowling and her trials getting Harry Potter published are encouraging, but do not take away that fear of being proved wrong.

Bromford prefer not to talk about 'wrong'. As soon as you mention the concept of blame you evoke the idea, so they talk about 'wobbly wheels'. Think of a supermarket trolley with those awful wheels – it is hard to keep them on track, they do not stop you doing your shopping, but they certainly do not help, and life is easier when they have been sorted out. Mistakes at Bromford are seen in this light – a wobbly wheel that needs to be attended to if we are to do our best work.

Bob Henry at CORGI does not speak of mistakes either, but 'unexpected outcomes'.

> We want people to take risks/be adventurous, not foolhardy, and we don't want them to be afraid of losing their job. It's OK if the outcome is unexpected – OK, but share it with others and look at what went on. If you repeat the behaviour and the outcome is the same, it's not unexpected any longer, and that's not acceptable – because you are not learning and we take a dim view of that. In that case we want to identify the development need that has to be addressed. Never start from the position that someone is setting out to do something wrong – why would they?

At Timpson it is very straightforward, according to James:

> Loads of people will say 'great idea' then never do it. We give everything a go, no matter how stupid it is. If it doesn't work, we put our hands up and say we've made a balls-up. When it does work, colleagues are asked to tell everyone about it so they can have a go themselves.

And so some great ideas are born.

Mistakes haunt people – their memory lingers well after the delights of a success. The temptation to hide them away can be compelling, pretending they never happened or hoping they will go away. Wragge have a mechanism for addressing this – Mental Block Day. Screen savers herald its arrival and encourage everyone to bring out their 'monster' files – the ones that sit at the bottom of the heap in the hope they will disappear from sight. Equally, when change was rife, taking the firm from its traditional legal style to the more individual style of 'Wragge, the great company', those who lagged behind were offered a 'dinosaur amnesty'. The senior partner came into work on Saturday to meet those who wanted to talk through the changes and their concerns, in the hope of both learning from them and bringing them on board.

Rather than thinking of mistakes, see different reactions or outcomes that contain valuable learning. It is questionable whether it is possible to create anything new unless it fails first. Could Honda produce such customer- and environmentally-friendly cars if they did not understand what does not work? Robert Hiscox, having worked for 40 years in the insurance business, has seen many ideas come and go – and come back again. He knows people have to give their ideas a try, even when they did not work before. This may just be the time it goes right or be the time to take the learning from it to move forward more effectively. His task is to hold off from saying that he had 'told them so' and to support their learning. No company can do without its mistakes.

'That could have gone horribly wrong – it's a big risk to put people into new roles unless you know they will be good enough.'
To quote Voltaire: 'Doubt is an uncomfortable condition, but certainty is a ridiculous one.'

It is great if you can be certain of an outcome, but that is not realistic in change. It all hinges on how you view mistakes. If you want a company to grow and develop, you need the courage to get out there – and if you do that, there will be times when you fail. It is inevitable – unless you are Superman. Unless you risk failure you are not changing – and not to change in this fast-paced world is the real risk. Standing still is the kiss of death.

Fear of mistakes is often to do with hierarchy and power. Mindsets about being right, pleasing people and not showing yourself up, stop action – better to be safe than sorry. Great companies change the mindset because they understand the limitation it creates. They want colleagues to seek out changes that benefit the business; they encourage people to learn from what works and does not work and to celebrate success as well as useful failure.

Action steps
Choose one action you are personally avoiding through fear of failure:

- Make an honest appraisal of the likely outcomes and the risks involved. Include the cost of not trying.
- Consider what is the worst that can happen and make a judgement – do the benefits outweigh the risks? If the answer is 'No', begin again with another action you have on hold.
- Work out a plan of action, including ways of supporting yourself – for example, talk to your boss and get agreement for your plan.
- Identify clear success factors – include unexpected outcomes that bring interesting learning.
- Celebrate your success with colleagues and share your learning.

Choose one action that your team are avoiding through fear of failure:

- Get the team together and work out a plan that provides optimum support for those taking the risk. Include clear measurements, timelines and checkpoints.
- Make it clear that you will not penalise failure – everyone will be concerned that you will react in a negative way if it does not work.
- If you need to, talk your own boss through the plan and get support for your actions.
- Let your agreed definition of success be the agreed outcome, a better outcome, or learning for the future.
- Celebrate the success you gain in a way that includes everyone involved.

The benefits of challenge

With an agreed approach on mistakes, there is the chance to put people into challenging situations to see what happens. There are two benefits to this. First of all, people are kept on their toes, given the responsibility to think in new ways and listen to new ideas. A common theme in talking to great company colleagues is that they are never given the chance to be bored. 'Before I get to that stage, I have been offered the next challenge.' This is fantastic management – that ability to spot the first murmurings of stagnation and change the game. 'People-handling brilliance affects productivity,' according to Asda.

Honda are expert at this, moving people around the business at regular intervals. People do not have time to settle down, unless that is what they want to do – after all, a company full of stars would be a nightmare. However, those who are ambitious are placed in new situations to stretch their thinking and keep them learning. There are no career plans; it is up to each person to take the chances as they arise. But there are also no limits as to what is possible, so sitting in the motorbike team and longing to work with cars is a problem that is easily solved. Find the job that needs to be done and ask for it.

Which brings us to the second advantage of moving people into new challenges. One risk in a great company is that people stay for a long time. It is brilliant on a number of fronts – the culture is maintained, recruitment costs are low, and expertise remains in the organisation. However, there is a risk of losing the impact of new blood and ideas from other companies. Dynamism requires disturbance – too much continuity can spell complacency. Change is scary, but it is also stimulating and enlivening. New thinking switches on the brain, lights up the thinking and ideas come storming through. Wise words from a colleague, Andrew Pearson, stick with me: 'Don't worry that those you train leave, but that those you don't train, stay.'

Moving people from one department to another is the internal equivalent of bringing in new blood. Bromford send people on sabbaticals to try a job, giving both challenge and stability – if the job does not work out, there is somewhere to go back to. They also use external assignments to bring new thinking back into the office. Asda encourage risk – so much so that some people do not want a job that is familiar. At St Luke's, account directors have become creatives and vice versa: finding the job that suits the talent is the big driver, never mind what your original title was.

'If people are given all this responsibility and challenge, they may become hard to manage.'

Yes they will, if being outspoken, direct and honest is hard to manage. If, as a manager, you like to maintain control, this is not the work style for you. Think it through. If you have full control over your team or department, progress is limited to your capacity for new ideas and strategic thought. If your team take responsibility, you can go as far as the team can visualise – the bar is raised by putting all heads together. This is the basis of employing the best people. To quote Robert Hiscox: 'Employ people brighter than you are. It raises your game and the whole business to a new dimension.'

This means losing some control – as the limits extend, you no longer have full knowledge and say about what is happening. If you try to take it back, your team will become disillusioned, so you need to find a different way of managing.

Action steps

Health warning: if you need to remain in control, think very carefully before you give additional responsibility – do not attempt it if you are not prepared to follow through.

- Select a project/work task that you are prepared to hand over.
- Talk with the team about the best way to take this forward. Clarify that they have the knowledge and information to do the work, or are willing to learn.
- Whatever you choose to do, do it wholeheartedly. Be clear who will have responsibility, and give a clear outline of the process.
- Work out the measures, timelines and checkpoints that will support you and the team in ensuring that the best work is done. Handing over responsibility is a poisoned chalice unless the parameters are clear – make sure that you are not setting yourself and others up to fail by giving incomplete information or support.
- Be clear about your role. Where does your responsibility lie, and when do you need to be consulted?
- Set regular reviews in place at team meetings to assess how it is working. Encourage honest feedback at all times. If you struggle to handle this, arrange some personal coaching to help you clarify your role and expectations.
- Be clear how you will view mistakes. People will not take risks if they expect a punitive response.
- Clarify what constitutes success, including the unexpected outcomes, and celebrate accordingly.

Leaders have as much responsibility for their own development as every other person in the organisation, and doing this effectively will contribute to a positive disturbance factor. Meeting leaders from other companies, going on leadership development programmes and executive coaching are all ways of taking a fresh look at the day-to-day. Nick claims that this is one of the driving forces in the great culture at Bromford, as does Bob Henry at CORGI. No one is immune, and providing a good role model right from the top is the perfect way to embed the importance of learning.

Remember: giving people responsibility for challenge, new direction and exploration is only one part of it. They must also have the support they need to do the job well – this is definitely not the time for abdication (see Table 3 above). Great company managers spot the moment, put in the challenge, and then give all the support needed until the person is up and running. To challenge and desert is business suicide – challenge as a joint venture is a sign of greatness.

Measurement

What gets measured gets done. At Asda they 'measure everything that moves, lives and breathes'. This underlines the fact that great companies are not just about creating nice places to come to each day. They are solid and very successful businesses that track carefully and thoroughly the work they do and the goals they are reaching for.

Everyone has to know exactly what they must achieve for the company to be successful. Colleagues with clear measures to work to know where they stand. They will spot more quickly when things are not going well, giving them the chance to make the necessary changes. They have clear parameters within which to act and to explain where they need help and support, and why.

This also forms the basis of useful appraisal. Setting measures that track outputs plus understanding fully the behaviours that underpin the achievement of the measures is the way to assess effectiveness in both productivity and management ability. This is how companies identify the great managers – by assessing the success of the team/direct reports as well as the manager himself or herself. (See the fifth 'case study' – *Responsibility requires clear measures* – at the end of this chapter.)

This is the big difference in how great companies use measurement. When numbers are down, the response is not just to put on the pressure and expect change to occur as a result. It is to wonder what is happening in the team: how come they are not able to achieve their targets? What is the problem? How can we help? If the reason is genuine under-performance, then the right action must be taken and not brushed under the carpet. (See the third 'case study' – *Facing the tough decisions* – at the end of Chapter 6.)

But measuring has another function: it is a wonderful way to ensure celebration of success. Without clear measures there is no way to determine when the outcome is reached. The goalposts can keep changing, precluding the excitement of achievement.

Add in honest and open feedback and you have the final piece for making challenge an excellent development tool. Responsibility for action, setting clear measures, supporting and providing straight feedback means that people know where they are, know what to expect and are more likely to take on further responsibility when the opportunity arises.

Great companies are places of learning, and learning is most effective when coupled with experience. Give people jobs to do, evaluate, discuss, measure, give feedback on what is going well and not so well, and you have the best university life can offer.

Summary

- Responsibility shows respect, develops skill and ability, while building a sense of belonging in the organisation.
- Look for real-time opportunities that will challenge and excite people. Learning through experience is highly effective and also brings new 'out of the box' thinking into the work.
- Trust is a prerequisite, since mistakes are inevitable and necessary for growth. Redefine success as the agreed outcome, as an alternative and better outcome, or as information that takes us to a better outcome. Optimise mistakes by understanding and learning from what happened.
- Ensure regular appraisals: once a year is not enough.
- See yourself as servant to your team – your job is to build an environment in which they can do their best work.

Give plenty of permission

Keep listening for new ideas. When you hear one, set your boundaries and let the instigators explore them further. Work on the basis of 'education, not blame', and watch people and the company grow.

Shortly after Richard arrived at Hiscox they opened regional offices. 'I know from my previous work that offices just don't talk to each other, so I suggested we install video-conferencing facilities.' The norm in London is to have regular meetings attended by everyone on site to update on company issues. Regional offices could so easily get left out of the loop and have no chance to ask questions. Not everyone was keen on the idea, but Richard told them, 'Trust me, you need to get their buy-in. It's not as good as being in the room, but better than nothing.'

He was sent off to investigate and produce a paper with costs, availability, etc. In due course he presented it to the relevant people and the idea was taken up. In fact, it has recently been upgraded. Now it helps in all sorts of ways. For example, reviewing new risks used to be done in individual offices, but now the company can put together a combination of underwriting minds at the regular monthly meeting.

This is not unusual at Hiscox, who embed the concept of supported challenge from the moment a new colleague arrives. When Sue Langley took up her job as Group operations director, she met with Bronek Masojada, Group CEO, to find out about her objectives, goals, timelines, and so on. He told her she had just one objective – 'to sort it out. Let me know what you decide is right and I will back you.' He also made a point of telling the board the same thing, so that everyone knew he was behind her and trusted her judgement. It confirmed her experience at interview that here was a place where she would be shown respect and valued for what she had to bring. A number of years later she has created vast change in the systems and is part of a highly effective leadership team, for whom she has great admiration.

Action steps

- Listen thoroughly to ideas from colleagues. Being on the front line, they will see issues that you cannot.
- People live up to expectations. If you trust and encourage people to follow through on ideas, they are more likely to succeed. Watch their every move and you will lose the people or, at the very least, the ideas.
- Demonstrate your intention by informing others. Everyone knows where they stand and you will affirm your belief in the person concerned.

Everyone makes mistakes

Mistakes are inevitable so it is best to expect them. It is also the best way of learning – you can guarantee the antennae will be highly sensitised another time! A colleague's first mistake is the critical one: how you respond as a manager will affect how willing the colleague is to take any risk in the future.

Andrew made his first mistake at Wragge after four months. Putting in the bills for completion of a deal, he found his calculation differed from what the client was expecting by £50,000. All he could think was that he had made a mistake in terminology, between what was said and what was written.

I could feel the blood draining from my face. I went straight to the partner concerned, who realised something was wrong from one look at me. Mark was great. He worked through it with me, dropping everything to give me the support I needed. He reassured me that I should not be concerned about negligence claims – that far worse than this could happen.

Five years on, Andrew still recalls the horror of realising what he had done. But the positive response from his partner means that he has been able to work on without constantly watching his back. Like the blue-chip CEO who chose not to sack a colleague who lost a large sum of money: 'Why would I sack you? I've just spent £500,000 training you!' Andrew is probably the very best person to work on clarifying contracts – he knows exactly what to look for.

Action steps

- Do not expect to be exempt – everyone makes mistakes, even you. Value them for the learning they bring.
- Be prepared to give time to people who know they have made a mistake. Not only do they need to understand what has happened, they will feel wretched and need your support. No one makes a mistake on purpose, so be understanding.
- If exactly the same thing happens again, investigate fully to see what has happened and work out a development plan for moving forward.
- If it happens for a third time, take appropriate action.

Being a role model

Leaders and managers have a responsibility to provide a positive role model in the workplace. Do not expect people to do as you say if you do not do it yourself.

At Bromford, leaders make a point of working and playing alongside colleagues regularly – whether in the workplace, on social occasions, or at charity events. Not only does this provide time to talk in a more informal way, it also indicates respect and a desire to understand life from another person's perspective.

As a manager you have a responsibility to your people. You must make an effort to build a relationship and be approachable – how else will you get to hear of great ideas or mistakes as they occur? By staying on at the annual Bromford Bash longer than he would normally have done, Nick realised how important it is to be seen outside of the business.

It's connecting not just as colleagues but as people. To begin with I wasn't that good at it. I was not prepared to spend a few minutes more to have a chat.

It was his own personal development work that persuaded Nick to explore this area more.

I took more of a personal look at how I was operating and what I wanted to get out of work. My work/life balance was poor. I was very task-oriented. I thought that others working long hours was good – I was out of balance. It was about sorting out my life priorities.

What he realised was that as long as he modelled such a driven lifestyle, no one else could have a balanced work and home life. They lived life like the leader – this was the way to get attention and respect.

Action steps

- Take responsibility for your own behaviour and effectiveness as a manager. As a role model you will have a major impact on the running of the business – so make sure you are a good one.
- Build relationships with your people and create an environment of trust so they can be honest at all times. This is the only way to guarantee that you hear what you need to hear.
- Keeping working on your own personal development. Not only will this ensure that you are working to full potential, it will demonstrate the importance of learning to everyone around you.

Encouraging feedback

Everyone in your business has knowledge that can help you move forward. Unless you make it clear that you want to hear, you will miss out on numerous ideas and solutions.

In the first week of his graduate placement in Honda, Gavin and his colleagues met with Ken Keir, the MD. 'You are not yet touched by Honda, so you are the closest we have here to a customer. Talk to us about your impressions.' Quite a challenge to a young man new to a job and itching to make a good impression – how honest should he be? Taking Ken at his word, Gavin told of the leaving gift from his previous job in a pharmaceutical company – a blue wig and a chamois leather, indicating a common perception of Honda cars.

Ken took the opportunity to affirm that they needed this sort of bluntness.

We have to attract the younger generation – help us with it. I'll soon be 60, so I don't have the right ideas. It's you guys who can generate ideas for the future.

This has had an enormous impact on Gavin and his peers. That the MD was to keen to hear his view even in the first week gave him permission to really go for it.

Louise had a similar experience of being thrown in at the deep end. In her first three months she was asked to redraw the dealership map of the UK. It meant reshuffling and re-organising the previous operation and presenting her results to senior leaders. Her plan is now in place – a massive achievement for one so new.

From the outset I felt I would be listened to and could make a difference. Everyone

> wanted one of the graduates – we were in high demand.
>
> The moral of the tale, according to Louise?
>
> Have confidence in your people and show it. Give them a free rein and don't be too rigid. They'll work better if they have time away from the mundane – let them take the company forward.

Action steps

- Be prepared to ask questions of colleagues at every level. Everyone has something to offer.
- Let newcomers know from the outset that their view is welcomed and you will embed good communication and respect.
- Give responsibility freely and back up with support – the result will be stimulated people, great ideas and a dynamic culture.

Responsibility requires clear measures

Measures and definitions of success provide boundaries within which to work. If you want experimentation, exploration and the best outcome, people must understand what is required and acceptable. If you do not do this, you set them up to fail and they learn not to take risks.

At Flight Centre (FC) measurements relate to tangible factors and form the Key Performance Indicators (KPI) for the company. 'Incentives are based on quantitative outcomes, particularly profit, profit increase, turnover increase, staff retention, numbers of staff developed (leaders), and net income.'

It sounds a far cry from what people imagine is a great people culture, but think about it. How are all those measures achieved? Through effective leadership, care of colleagues, creativity and innovation, and personal and team development. All too often we forget that it is people who run a business – without them there is no profit.

Ninety per cent of FC colleagues sell travel, so if they are doing right by customers, and focusing on cost control, the net result is profit. Money is an easy measure, but it will not do on its own. As other companies have found to their cost, money still comes in for a while after standards have dropped – customers keep hoping it will improve. Poor service now will impact on the bottom line in a couple of years, by which time the rot has set in. So talking with customers on a regular basis and judging their reaction is a valuable indicator.

Staff vacancies is another measure – 'If the vacancy rate in the UK is less than 5 per cent, and in South Africa it's 10 per cent, then the UK's is clearly the better team.' We all know that people leave managers more often than they leave the job, so the leader must take full responsibility for creating an environment that people want to work in. Their bonus depends upon it.

Underlying each of the measures is the recognition of what is required to achieve it. Vacancy rates rely on good leadership and the work environment, customer service relies on colleagues taking responsibility, profit is only produced when people feel included through effective communication and develop a strong sense of commitment and belonging. All the elements come together to create a positive bottom line.

Measures work well – as long as we remember that they are an outcome. Building on what produces them creates a great company.

Action steps

- Do not issue instructions or threats to stimulate improvement – this drives people underground or increases stress, reducing effectiveness.
- If numbers are down, talk with the team to find out what is happening and listen to their concerns. Find out what other problems they are facing, and what you must do to improve the environment so they can work more effectively. Provide support for those who are struggling.
- Examine your own concerns about measurement: the effectiveness of your work will be clear, which can be scary. Address your concerns and look to upskill in the areas in which you have least confidence.
- Get the help you need to prepare for the honest conversations that are part of the process – talk to the HR department or your manager about working with a coach. Giving and taking feedback is never easy, yet if the matter is left to chance, the business will suffer.

Chapter 9

Building a sense of belonging

If you want me as a loyal member of your company, you have to build a strong sense of belonging. If I don't feel included, why would I stay?

For someone like Geraldine Allinson, associate director of Kent Messenger Group, it is easy. She is the fourth generation to work in the business since 1859.

It's my family business. The Chairman is my father. I came to help out when the print union strikes hit us, just prior to Wapping, and I got the bug. I was supposed to study geography at university, but changed to do a business degree instead. After working on another newspaper group for experience, I came to KM, and I just love it.

Describing work as being like family is not uncommon in great companies and many organisations go out of their way to cultivate the culture experienced at Kent Messenger and Timpson. Those companies have a head start, since they really are family, but they still have to address the issue of building belonging for new people.

Flight Centre have been conscious of this need. Their structure breaks people into families (teams), villages (geographical teams that support each other) and tribes (areas). Couple this with their Statement of Egalitarianism and Unity in the Workplace:

In our company we believe that every individual should have equal privileges. We will never have separate offices, receptionists or secretaries. Promotion from within will always be our first choice. We believe that work should be challenging and fun for everyone. Within our company there is no 'them and us'. We are all going forward together.

This is an exceptionally strong, inclusive statement and one that is played out in reality day by day.

Family at its best carries a strong feeling of belonging. Something in the blood tie elicits caring, despite different personalities and needs.

However strained relationships become, true families rally round in the bad times. They applaud success and are thrilled for us at those exciting turning points in life, pulling out all the stops to make sure we get what we need. Family is also a place of great challenge – when no one else will tell the truth, a sibling or parent will take us gently on one side for that difficult conversation, and it is not easy to get away with bad behaviour. Ensuring that children have a safe, healthy and secure life ahead is a strong driver to parents, leading to all those demands for hard work and endeavour that drive teenagers wild.

I do realise that this is idealistic and that not everyone is fortunate enough to have a family that provides and supports in this way. However, we all deserve and need it. Human beings are communal creatures we want companionship and need to be included in a group with whom we feel at one. As more families become dispersed over the globe, so friends and work increasingly fill the gap. Which brings us back to great companies.

Inclusion at work

The edge great companies have is that they provide, in a work setting, some of the inclusion needs of colleagues. A company or organisation will never replace the family unit, but the friendships and commitment formed during the working day go a long way towards filling the gap.

Jason describes Wragge & Co. as being like his family.

> I am chuffed to say I work here. It's a bit like being a sibling – even when I was cross with my brother, I would never let anyone else talk badly of him. It is the same with Wragge – outsiders have me to deal with if they criticise us.

And why does he feel like that? Because Wragge 'goes the extra mile' for him and he is 'at one' with the principles.

There are countless stories of people who have hit difficult times and been supported by the company. Of unexpected deaths after which people have been given as much time off as they needed, regardless of the designated allowance. Of Timpsons, who lend money to colleagues in debt, rather than risk them getting involved with loan sharks. Of the young Honda employee who was let down by the wedding chauffeur at the last minute and was given the president's limo for as long as he needed it. When the caring side of a culture is strong, the company will step into the breach.

An employee at Kent Messenger Group discovered she had cancer. She told her boss, who then communicated it to the board.

> At the end of their meeting they all came in to see me one by one, closed the door and sat down to give me a bit of encouragement. I just thought, 'This is a lovely place. People really care about each other.' I see this a lot around the company.

But concern does not always lead to a great workplace. It can be paternalistic and therefore limiting. Parents generally care, but there is a world of difference between those who care but believe their way to be the only right way, and those who support us in doing things in our own style. Paternalistic organisations will certainly show care and step up to the plate when needed, but they can also be demanding in a way that is deeply limiting to human potential. When gratitude is required or guilt played upon, the relationship is unhealthy and unequal. People stay because they feel they should or because they have lost self-esteem to such a point that they do not believe they could go elsewhere. When this happens, you have a caring company – you do not have a great company.

Remember the unity statement of Flight Centre: *we are all going forward together*. That means we do what is right for the one in need, not what is right for the giver. Great companies are like family – but in a grown-up way. People are responsible for themselves within the context of the whole and they are expected to do what is right for themselves, other colleagues and the organisation.

How to create belonging

Getting the right people is clearly a major part of the process, but unless you have a positive environment for them to come to, they are unlikely to stay.

> 'Not every company can afford the posh surroundings of the blue-chips. Does that mean people won't stay?'
> Absolutely not. There are some exceptionally smart workplaces out there that do not have great company culture and that lose people on a regular basis. Make the very best of what you have, and ensure that the environment is appropriate, so that colleagues are comfortable doing their work. You can more than make up for the glitz through strong relationships and respect.

Action steps

Complete a thorough assessment of the physical working environment:

- Do people have enough space for their work? If they are cramped, is there a way to reorganise that will make better use of the space available? If not, put the issue of office space on the next management meeting agenda and brainstorm alternatives.
- Is the office warm in winter and cool in summer? Is there natural light and air in the room?
- Do the chairs provide a good seating position, with desks at the right height?
- Is there a comfortable room for people to go to on their break, with access to hot drinks and water?
- Is the building clean and well cared for?

If you have funds to make improvements in the environment, ask your people the following questions:

- How do you rate the work environment at present? What is good about it? What does not work well?
- Given that we have a limited resource for change, what are the features that would make the most difference to your working day?

Once you have clear feedback, consider the following:

- Set up a colleague working party to address the changes. Encouraging colleagues to be part of the process will ensure that you make the best use of the funds available.
- Give the working party a float to spend as it sees fit. This ensures that people are proactive and take the responsibility to act directly on some issues without having to confer with management.
- Ensure that you have a clear communication process for changes you choose to put in place: regular meetings to give information about changes planned; question-and-answer facilities on both sides to determine the best way forward; suggestions boxes for ideas to add to your management discussions.

The more you include people in decisions about their daily working environment, the more likely you are to make a significant difference.

Fair deal

To attract and keep the right people you must offer a fair deal. Everyone needs money. We all need enough to keep ourselves and those dear to us in the manner we consider appropriate. Companies have different ways of doing this, from competitive salaries to reasonable base salary and bonus. The latter is the choice of those companies that actively encourage entrepreneurial attitudes. At Flight Centre everyone runs their own business, taking bonus on all income once their 'cost of seat' is covered. Managers can also buy shares in their own shop if they wish. The outcome is that people make as much money as they need because they are in charge. If you have ever run your own business or taken total responsibility for a project, you know how much this affects your commitment. Not only do you want to do well financially, you also want to do a job you can be proud of – so yet again everyone wins.

For those on ordinary salary, it is true that not every great company pays brilliantly, but what is really important is that they are fair. It is a dreadful feeling to be taken advantage of, and no one works well under those conditions. This is true on all levels, but money is often the easiest means of identifying when you feel mistreated. When people understand the reasoning behind salary decisions, or there are enough other advantages to make a job worthwhile, they accept what they are given.

You should also set this against those companies that pay really well and yet have negative people cultures. No amount of money will make up for the loss of self-esteem caused by working with an inept or neglectful manager. The worst thing about this is that when the money is very good, it is hard to leave. Life expands to spend the money available and it is hard to imagine cutting back for the sake of happiness – fear and uncertainty play all sorts of tricks, resulting in 'golden handcuffs' and depression.

In that context, the slightly lower income earned by Asda shop assistants is less important, compared to the pleasure they gain from working there. They are really well cared for, to the point of grandparent's leave and to the extent that colleagues who want a long winter break have been sent on 'Benidorm leave' for a few months. Money will go a long way to making people happy, but once they have a sufficiency, other elements kick in. The positive glow created by an employer who thinks about you and provides perks that make life easier or more fun cannot be bought with a few extra pounds a month.

Provision of benefits is another way for companies to show their respect and concern for colleagues. More than just a way of beating the competition, they also make sense in terms of having a healthy and motivated workforce. The fact that AstraZeneca provides a well-being facility at its Charnwood site, including fitness equipment that people can visit during the working day, is one way to encourage colleagues to maintain a healthy lifestyle. From the same mindset, companies provide massage, doctors on site, dry-cleaners and money machines, access to online shopping – the list is endless.

'This sounds expensive! Not every company has that much money to spend.'

First, get your priorities right. Ensure that you offer the best benefits package possible with regard to pension, health care, maternity/paternity leave, etc. This is one differentiator for new recruits – they want to know they will be well looked after in exchange for their hard work. It is also a sign that the company will care for them.

Benchmark yourself against other companies. You can find some information on websites. Non-competing companies may be willing to tell you what they offer, if you ask them. Talk with friends and colleagues from other organisations and find out what benefits they receive.

- If you do not work in the HR department, write down your findings and present a case for re-evaluating the company package.

Second, look at the local possibilities that can be leveraged. Remember that you have a captive audience and that other businesses may be interested in serving your people.

- Ask local dry-cleaners if they will collect and deliver.
- Allow time for people to order their supermarket shopping on-line and take delivery at work; it will take minimum time out of the day.
- Speak to the local bank to see if it will provide an ATM machine. If its own business will benefit, it may cost the company little while providing a service for colleagues.

Third, look through the *Sunday Times* supplement for the *100 Best Companies to Work For* or look on the *Sunday Times* website and see if there are any good ideas you can pinch. Many initiatives cost little, are very inclusive, and build a strong sense of team and belonging:

- dress-down day once a week
- bring-your-pet-to-work day
- set up a social committee to plan regular events
- bring-your-daughter/son-to-work day
- install a machine that makes really good coffee
- bring together all the pregnant parents and ask the local midwife to come and talk to them
- provide a birthday cake on the closest working day.

Speak to people to find out what they would like to do. You do not have to read their minds – just ask.

Families at work

More women want to remain in the workplace these days, and more leaders perceive the value women bring to the business environment. Couple this with the trend for men to be more active fathers and you have created a need for better maternity, paternity and childcare provision at work. Great companies recognise and relish this, not least because the inclusion of actual family in the realm of the business increases that sense of belonging. When the organisation is positive about children and the demands they make, it is more likely that a working mum will return to work, keeping her expertise and her experience of clients in the business. All these measures are good for colleagues and increase the attraction of the company – but let us be clear, they also serve the business very well.

Where funds allow, companies provide childcare on the premises – a big attraction to working mums. If that is too expensive an option, it is still possible to make links with local childcare providers and oil the wheels of getting care organised. Also be aware that childcare may go wrong and that kids may fall ill. Managers who trust colleagues, encouraging them to get things sorted out before thinking of coming back to work, earn huge loyalty and commitment. Of course there will be some people who try to take advantage of this level of flexibility, but knowing your people will help you to nip this in the bud.

Flexible working

Which brings us to flexible working generally. This is not new to most great companies, who have already identified this as a positive advantage to the workforce and the business. Legislation is bringing other companies on board by ensuring that parents/carers can work flexibly to cater to the needs of children and dependants. However, limiting this right to carers is a risk – there are many unfettered workers out there who would love to work different hours in order to enjoy some rest and recreation or to follow a particular hobby. Companies that recognise this are on the way to keeping a very happy workforce without the underlying niggles of inequality.

The levels of trust inherent in great company culture mean that the essence of flexible working will have been in place for a long time and it does not need the government to tell the company it is the right thing to do. When you trust a person, you know that they will get a job done, so you adjust the timing to suit their needs. Some places have also found this to be a business advantage, enabling them to give the customer greater flexibility. Life is made considerably easier by adjusting time, providing childcare on or near the premises, and having an understanding boss who knows full well that sports day is a major event and that emergencies will inevitably arise. Equally, the boss who realises that taking time out in the middle of the day to watch Wimbledon in June, catching up on work in the evening or starting early because you are an early riser, will make work more suited to having a good life.

Fun as part of the working day

The practical side of being a big family is only part of the equation. In the light of how much time we spend at work, it is a great pity if we do not manage to have fun. This is a very interesting area in great company philosophy. It is all too easy to assume a definition of fun, when in fact it is something that changes from person to person and from company to company. And it perfectly demonstrates that a company is only great if the people working there think it is. You and I looking from the outside can make a guess at it, but will never really know unless we ask those involved. Companies are made up of people who are all totally different, so each organisation must look for its personal signature.

From the fun perspective, it is a matter of understanding what colleagues enjoy – so what better way than to involve them in creating the enjoyable interludes. At St Luke's each person receives the annual 'Make yourself more interesting' fund – £150 per person to use in an interesting way. Activities range from Indian head massage, kick boxing and philosophy, to swimming with dolphins, providing fascinating reports back to the company. Each newcomer is also given £100 when he or she joins, to buy a present for the agency. After working there a while, a group of new starters clubbed together to buy patio heaters for the deck outside the restaurant doors. Now they can have barbecues more frequently.

Asda have a monthly meeting at Asda House in Leeds that gives the latest company information in a fun way, generally accompanied by some interesting celebrity appearance – like having Atomic Kitten to sing to them. Of course, fun does not have to take huge budgets – at Honda it is getting the chance to have a go on the bikes and the little racing cars built with lawnmover engines; at Timpson it is all getting together over a pint funded by James Timpson; and at Wragge it can be sleeping out overnight to raise money for the homeless. It is a matter of finding out what people want and what the company can afford in terms of time and money, and then getting on with it.

In so many companies, work is what is important and fun is something you have when you leave. But that really is missing the point. Think of the last time you had a good time. Sharing a laugh or a sense of satisfaction binds people together. Those times you laughed till you cried over a good joke, or shared a good natter over a glass of wine, build connections and can be the stuff of company stories – this is one way culture is built.

'Doesn't this make it difficult for people to concentrate on the work at hand? Too much fun can be a distraction and destroy a working day.'
You need to keep a balance. It does not have to be a funfair, just an environment in which people can have a laugh together and in which success is celebrated. Taking a break can be just the thing to raise a flagging spirit, where continuing against the odds can lead to mistakes.

Don't save fun for Christmas – make sure it has a regular presence in your team. Sharing fun together will improve effectiveness by building relationships and strengthening belonging.

- Make an assessment of fun in the workplace. Is there a balance of hard work and downtime?
- In your team, look for successes to celebrate – a small gift of

chocolates or doughnuts all round is a great way to validate a piece of work done well, while providing a break and a bit of fun.
- Make sure that you know what team members enjoy (see the Timpson test list in Chapter 6) – for instance, if someone loves their garden, a few bedding plants will go down much better than a standard box of chocolates, and show that you thought about them specifically.
- Get the team together over a coffee and talk with them about ways to have fun. You do not have to have all the answers, just the willingness to find out and allow the time.

Relationships with suppliers

Some organisations spread the net beyond colleagues to include suppliers. For many companies it is so important to stick to their principles that they will work only with companies that are aligned. This is one way of spreading the ethical worth of great companies, demonstrating total commitment to colleagues along the way. Asda are a prime example of this, demanding that suppliers adhere to the same set of principles if they wish to have a business relationship.

It is hard to have a strong set of principles in relation to how people are treated, and then connect with a company that puts money first. The underlying intentions will be different – through no fault of the people concerned – it is just a different ethos. Connections between companies where one has high levels of trust while the other is cynical and looking out for number one are extremely difficult. It is like trying to link a Pentium processor into an Amstrad – it will not work, and if it does manage to get moving, there will be all manner of misunderstandings. Each side is talking a different language. Deals done under these circumstances have a high risk of failure.

At TD Industries they began the business with agreements made on a handshake. The leaders were so highly regarded in the community that no one needed further confirmation. They have become more formal these days, but still if a TD person says work will be done, it will be done. Imagine then working with a supplier who does not offer a high level of reliability and integrity. The risks are enormous and untenable in some circumstances. There is then the choice either to change TD in a way that could be detrimental to the company culture or to work with suppliers who have equally high standards. The latter makes sense on all fronts, since to work with companies who do not believe in the care of people and who demonstrate low levels of integrity would be to condone their behaviour.

That Cisco Systems had such positive relationships with suppliers was a saving grace when the technology bubble burst. There was no choice but to make redundancies, given the major drop in the market, but it was a really tough call for a company that was so clear about caring for colleagues. The way out was to take on the work of an outplacement agency and approach suppliers to see what jobs they had available. The result was that the majority of people moved to work with those who were still considered part of the Cisco family.

This relationship begins the moment someone connects to a company. Through writing this book, I have become an expert on being welcomed into a building or into the life of the company over the phone. Receptionists and PAs are very significant people in great companies, acting as the first link to the outside world. They take the time to extend belonging to the caller – to have a chat, to get to know the person, makes sure that they get what they need.

My early contacts with Asda are a perfect example. After quite a struggle, Kate Wood, PA to the CEO, managed to find a time when I could meet with Tony DeNunzio and David Smith. Not realising they were located in Leeds, I agreed to meet them on my daughter's birthday, assuming I would easily be back to spend the evening with my family. It was with trepidation I rang Kate to tell her of the problem and her immediate response was to say, 'You obviously can't come on that day – I'll start again.' I immediately felt valued and included, something no amount of rhetoric could engender.

Never underestimate the importance of those first moments. We take it for granted that customer service requires a positive welcome, yet we must return again to colleague/supplier experience – we can only give what we receive. The skill of including others can only be demonstrated by those who feel included themselves.

The Great Company family

There is a whole new family emerging now as more companies are named as having great cultures. The desire for learning and the willingness to share means that companies contact each other to talk and benchmark together. Given the common theme of 'pinching ideas', it makes sense that they would speak and share learning.

It has been a fascinating experience to visit and talk with so many interesting companies. Each one opened its doors to me, enabled me to talk with whomever I wanted. They trusted me to represent them well and supported me in every way I needed. I have met some fantastic people, some face to face and some over the phone – I know about kids, holidays, GCSE results, and they know about me. The warmth created from being treated in this way is an accolade to each and every one of those people who are the face of the company.

Summary

- Make sure that everyone feels included by getting to know people and providing support and care when they face difficult times.
- Build a positive work environment – make sure that colleagues are physically comfortable and have all they need to do their job well.
- Offer the best pay and benefits you can. Benchmark against your competitors to see how you measure up. Above all, be fair.
- Be family-friendly and mindful of the extra pressures managed by working parents.
- Look into flexible working and offer it where you can. It can also produce definite benefits for the business.
- Make work a fun place to come to – it will help concentration and commitment.
- Include your suppliers in the 'family' of the company – it will improve the service you bring each other and cement a positive relationship.

Ideas for building belonging

CORGI: developing flexible working

Great companies understand the value of flexible working, both for colleagues and for the business.

When the government made it obligatory to offer flexible working to carers, CORGI sent round an e-mail to everyone. The company had offered this to colleagues for a long time, but they took this opportunity to put out a reminder.

Carol, a working mum with two kids, had been thinking for a while that she would really like to work part-time, but had been a little wary of broaching it to her boss. Encouraged by the e-mail she took the plunge. 'How soon do you want to start?' was the immediate response.

Bob Henry believed flexible working was the right thing to do for the people, but soon discovered that it was also the right thing to do for the business. Changing start and finish times to suit personal circumstances provides their customers with a much better service – colleagues can be available for a much longer working day. Couple this with colleagues who are better able to balance their work and home lives and you have a win all round.

Communication that shows you matter

Communication serves the business but also conveys how people are regarded. Being available is a mark of respect and underpins the equality of great workplaces.

Gary Hogan does not have a PA, and nor does anyone else at Flight Centre. This comes out of their guiding principle that everyone is equal, which means that everyone does their own 'grunt work' rather than expecting it to be done for them.

Prioritising has to be effective – you will not survive under these conditions if you take on too much and do not deliver on time. In the light of the fact that the company publishes its performance weekly and rewards success extremely well, this is no place for 'to do' lists that just grow ever longer. Which certainly serves to concentrate the mind and promote effective delegation.

Colleagues can speak directly to anyone from area manager to MD. Mobile numbers are available and call-back is within 24 hours. I had reason to call Gary recently and he really did do that – within the allotted time I had the response I needed.

Time is the most common reason for limiting availability. If you trust people and ensure that they can make contact when they need to, they will behave like grown-ups and not abuse the privilege. Because you are providing them with what they need to do a good job, they will show equal care for you.

Successful teamwork
Excellent teamwork means that people pull together to achieve a worthwhile task. Given respect and trust, they will set their own targets and provide a high-quality service.

So strong is Liz Walford's belief in the team, she

> can guarantee that the teams who have their targets displayed on the wall will be the top-performing teams – definitely. Sharing where the team is going and making it visible to others is a really strong statement of intent.

She told me of a team that set its own targets around numbers of houses empty at the year end – a significant measure in the housing arena, since each empty home means loss of income and the year-end snapshot is an industry benchmark measure.

In contrast to the Bromford Group's 'official' business plan target, the team set a 'big hairy goal'.

At year-end we normally had 30 to 40 empty homes. This team said it would have no empty homes. Although an eternal optimist, I really did think this was ludicrous and that they would never manage it.

But the team came in with a zero.

It was amazing, and the ripple effect was huge! For instance, success depended on the challenge being jointly owned by colleagues working in various parts of the business – housing teams and maintenance teams in this case. It led everyone to look at what happens when someone moves out of a property – getting the repairs done, finding the next person to move in, looking at every part of the process. We had been talking about that kind of cross-team working for a while, but it had all been a bit theoretical. The front-line colleagues' setting their own truly aspirational target revived everyone's interest in the business result we needed and in improving the process behind it.

And it didn't stop there – achieving the zero whetted people's appetite, so they decided to go for it at the end of each quarter – they 'raised their own high jump' and embedded the change into everyday activities. We now have much better results and for two years running have been the best in the country on that measure. I learned a lot from that team – they fundamentally changed my approach to target-setting.

Why would people take on a tougher job than they need to? It would have been easy to stick with the more limited target. Under the right circumstances it can be exciting to reach for a stretch target, finding out more about your limits – and when you all do it together, it becomes fun. Teams at Bromford built on the fun element to tackle the tough question of rent arrears. 'It's a tough job when people won't answer the door and don't answer the phone.' The team thought they might have more success contacting people later in the day – so they started some themed evenings. 'For instance, a pizza evening – something to make it fun to stay at work – to be there as a team, to get on the phones and work through a challenging task together.' So 'knock 'em dead with garlic bread' night was born, together with a really strong sense of belonging.

Real business ownership
Some companies offer share options or profit share to ensure that people take ownership of the company.

Giving shares or share options or operating profit share schemes are traditional ways of holding on to high-flying personnel. Some great companies carry this through to every employee to ensure that each person has a stake in the future of the business.

At Flight Centre, everyone is incentivised. The better they do, the more money they make, with no cap on the final amount. The result is a number of comparatively wealthy young people who would have had no chance of such high earnings in any other company at that age. Couple this with a superb track record of celebrating all that success and it is no wonder that they want to stay.

At Asda every colleague can be a shareholder once he or she has been in post for 12 months. There is also a discretionary bonus scheme so that managers can recognise good service and performance.

At TD Industries, as well as St Luke's, everyone is a shareholder. People take care of the company when they are part of it – you think twice about company expenses when it will affect your dividend at the end of the year.

Demonstrating trust
To trust is to give a real gift. You show people that you appreciate them, value their skill and integrity and care for their well-being. Such care is always repaid in some manner.

When Richard had been at Hiscox for about four months, another company made a bid to buy them.

> Rather than let rumours grow, Bronek and Robert called a meeting and told us all what had happened and let everyone ask the questions that were bothering them. They were probably sailing close to the wind with what they were sharing.

Clearly the leadership could not be totally democratic in their decisions about this issue, but they demonstrated beyond a doubt the level of trust they placed in their people.

At Richer Sounds, colleagues are given a bonus at the end of the week. Nothing unusual in this, except that they are encouraged to take it directly from the till so that they have some money to spend on a night out. This shows both immense trust and an understanding of the young, predominantly male workforce, for whom Saturday night is an important time.

People will step up when trusted. It improves the quality of the work while modelling a style of management and leadership that will lead to the building of trust throughout the organisation.

Action steps

- Be sure you understand your responsibilities in respect of flexible working. Talk with your HR department or go on to the website of the DTI for information. Find out what the options are for carers in your organisation and make sure your people know about them.
- Keep a record of how available you are to direct reports/colleagues. How long does it take you to return a call or answer a request for information or support? Can people speak to you direct when they need to? If not, look for ways to be more available.
- Include the team in setting objectives and goals. Listen to what they believe they can achieve. If it is below your expectation, have a discussion, put your point of view and reach agreement. The more you trust their judgement, the more likely they are to stretch.

Chapter 10

360-degree service: going the extra mile for everyone

I felt profoundly moved when Mark Davies at Honda described his job as a leader:

> You know that look in a person's eye when they are on a mission? It's my job to spot that and make the space around them so they can go for it.

This is servant leadership.

Service is more than just making sure that your customers are happy: that their calls are answered in three rings or less, or that they are always greeted with a smile. Service applies to all your stakeholders. In fact, in terms of your personal impact on the business, the service you offer to your staff and suppliers is at least as important as that which you offer to your customers.

Service means being present and active on behalf of another for their sake and not for your own. It means putting aside your own ego and personal gain so that someone else can succeed. Yet it is a glorious paradox — when you offer real servant leadership, you get back more than you put in because your business benefits from your team's success. But you have to give honestly. If you concentrate on the benefits you expect to get, the receiver will know and the impact is reduced.

Zen teachers speak of giving up attachment to the outcome. In Western terms this means putting the other person first. To quote John Crabtree at Wragge & Co: 'Cast your bread upon the water and it will come back a ham sandwich' (see the 'case study' at the end of Chapter 2). You must offer service to others in the belief that what you need will come back from somewhere, somehow. If you act only when you can see a direct result, you lose out.

Great companies approach their people with a sense of service. Bob Henry stopping at any time to talk to a person who needs help, is serving. Viv at Kent Messenger Group sitting down with an under-performer to understand how to help – this is service. As is the sundown rule at Asda where every request or concern from a shop is dealt with on the day it is received. The thrust is always to provide the best environment for each person to thrive. This is where the sparkle comes from, and is why each time I visit a company I feel inspired and excited. Everyone, including me, feels well cared for – well served.

360-degree service

There is only so much you can give unless you are cared for yourself. Depleted people have little to offer. In a feeling sense, they are on sur-vival rations – to maintain self-esteem they must look after themselves, believing that no one else will. 'Jobsworth' people are those who have little left to give. They have to get through the day, and your problem is just one too many for them.

Colleagues in great companies feel well respected and cared for. With employers who value the skills they bring and want to see them get ahead, they are rich in self-esteem. When things are not working – and they do not always work – they are strong enough to talk with bosses and colleagues to create change. They belong to something bigger and are better for it. And the result? It is a connection that should not surprise you. This level of service to, and regard for, colleagues makes great companies some of the best customer service organisations around.

Take Southwest Airlines: even in the recent tough times for the travel industry, they remain in the black – the only US airline to do so. This is due to the commitment of their people, who will do all they can to keep the company afloat. You may think this is self-evident – obvi-ously they want to keep their jobs – but it is not as simple as that.

The same thing happened in many organisations as the stock market plummeted and everyone was desperate to keep their jobs. But there is a difference – if the company has not cared enough, people feel depleted, have little to offer and are compelled to look after number one. At Southwest, where people are truly valued, they have energy in reserve for the company, so you hear stories of pilots who load bags rather than take a delay, which would cost money. Their customer service is exemplary, evoking huge loyalty, but colleagues could not do it if they felt ignored and undervalued by their leaders.

'It is not easy to maintain people as a priority when so many business demands cross your desk – how do you balance priorities?'

No one would say this is an easy task. It will always be tempting to close the door and get on with the demands of managing the business. Remember: the people you work with *are* the business – you cannot have one without the other. People management is part of the real job, not just an irritating addition.

Know your people, communicate clearly, and understand what they need in order to do a great job, and you will reduce the fire-fighting work you have to do. Good relationships make for trust, which improves delegation and overall effectiveness. Think how much time it takes when someone is doing a job badly – much better to make that time investment at the outset than pick up the pieces afterwards.

Make a point of recognising extra effort and pay attention to personal needs. Having an employer who understands when the kids are ill, or when you have financial difficulties, is worth so much. It needs to happen only once and that person – and all those who know about it – will respond with added loyalty.

What to do?

Look for the opportunity to support a person in your care. As John Timpson says of customer service, 'Each problem gives us a chance to amaze you.' The same goes for your people, so find ways to amaze them too – but make sure you really mean it. They will know the difference.

Talk with each person who reports to you and find out what they need in order to do a better job. Take care to listen more than talk during the discussion – this is a fact-finding mission, not the chance to tell people what to do.

Make sure you follow through on agreed actions. Asking without follow-through will cost more credibility than not asking at all.

Track how you spend your time. Make sure you are the best person for the job. If there is work that would be more appropriate for someone else in the team, or would be a good vehicle for development, set aside time to train and support that person. It will take time now, but save it in the future, not to mention the benefit to your relationship with that person.

Understand: the more involved you are with people, the more loyalty they will feel towards you. This is priceless in tough times, so invest now.

Once you have a community that lives by its principles and is prepared to support the well-being of another, the attitude of service begins to grow. It is all to do with the mindset – if people expect scarcity – ie to have to cope with the bare minimum – they will pull in their horns and look after themselves. A mindset of abundance, understanding there is good will and care in plenty, will allow them to look after each other because they have energy to spare. It is abundance that builds a great company and 360-degree service. Which means caring for peers and colleagues, the company, customers, and the community the organisation sits in. So it makes sense for everyone involved.

Providing the basics

The first step is to provide a good environment in which to work, plus a standard of living that fulfils personal needs. Many of the great companies are renowned for this, providing a plethora of wonderful perks and benefits – gyms, Indian head-massage, shopping on-line – anything that will make people feel better, healthier, and less stressed. This is not just altruistic: healthy colleagues give more to the job, so it makes sound business sense. (See Chapter 9 on Belonging for more detail.)

Moneywise and Healthwise are facilities put in place by Flight Centre to ensure that their young colleagues take care of themselves over the long term. In one-to-ones managers discuss where you want to go in life, and whether you will need a house, a car, or want to travel. 'Brightness of Future' – part of the company vision – is not just about work, it is about what work can bring you. Buying a first house and owning your first high-quality car are turning points that require an understanding of money and planning. Moneywise provides basic information about credit cards, mortgages, insurance, etc through an independent financial adviser, paid for by the company, who negotiates good deals on the basis of company buying-power.

Healthwise is a similar service that drip-feeds information through daily hotlines providing ideas on fitness and dietary issues – including how to handle a hangover after a 'buzz night'! As Gary says:

> It may seem like a tangent but is critical to looking after our consultants. If they feel good about themselves, secure and cared for, there's a good chance they'll treat the customer with equal respect. If we treat them like dirt, they'll do the same thing. We start from within.

Wragge worked out an interesting way of encouraging colleagues to look after themselves. The personnel team in the HR department instigated a 'well-being day' to launch the new Employee Assistance programme. Knowing that if the information was just sent round in an e-mail or letter, people would not absorb what was on offer, they decided to take the opportunity for a fun event. Wragge have a wonderful old banking-hall in their building, and this was the perfect setting for a gathering. The personnel team contacted people in the town to see if they would be willing to offer their services – a win/win that means celebrations do not have to cost a fortune. The end result was a fair of providers offering everything from fresh smoothies to neck massage. It was so successful that it has been put in the calendar for next year.

Reward and recognition

Once people have their physical needs answered, they begin to look elsewhere for appreciation and satisfaction. This is where reward and recognition comes in. Asda have 'Oscars night' to reward the Colleague of the Year – mimicking the real thing down to the red carpet, limos and evening dress. The senior leaders even dress up as celebrity characters – I have to tell you that Tony DeNunzio makes an extremely impressive Freddie Mercury!

This is not just a 'nice to have' for colleagues. What gets measured gets done and if what is done is also rewarded, there is a major impetus to success. So the many versions of awards and rewards come into being, providing a chance for celebration and fun, as well as demonstrating that success is highly valued. Bottles of champagne, vouchers for a spending spree, 'take your partner out for a meal' vouchers, handwritten notes, announcements in the team meeting, the senior manager or CEO popping over to say 'Well done' – all these are ways of giving a strong message that colleagues are valued and appreciated.

Each month, as mentioned above, Flight Centre areas hold a 'buzz night' – an evening when everyone gets together to learn, celebrate success and have a good time. Learning is from the company providers – airlines, hotel chains, etc – who come to tell of new offerings. There is one condition: they have to do it in the FC way and make it fun, which means they look forward to the evenings as much as the staff! The next stage is giving out awards. FC measure everything, so there is always much to be rewarded – best consultant, best new consultant, best customer appreciation – and so it goes on. Once this is completed it is down to the serious business of partying. Everyone is expected to attend – something that is made clear at interview, but that in fact needs little coercion – it is just too much fun.

'What if that sort of celebration doesn't fit your people – how do you go about finding the right way for them?'

Let us just go back to part of the definition of a great company – that it is a place where they tailor responses to suit their own colleagues. This is not about forcing fun down people's throats. Flight Centre has a young staff group that loves to travel and have fun – a buzz night is just right for them. Bromford have their annual 'bash' with entertainment provided by the senior team who put on a topical skit. In contrast, at CORGI colleagues gain most pleasure from the work itself, sharing their delight in the moment. However, they do occasionally look at the company opposite who are rather raucous in their celebrations and wonder if they could have a bit more fun themselves.

Constantly asking those sorts of questions is the key – understand what your people like to do. What is a reward and incentive for them? What makes them feel appreciated and cared for?

This is not as easy as it sounds – beware of assuming that everyone likes the same things you do. But do make the effort to find out and then take the time to party together in their way. It may be lunch at the pub or a family day out or, as at Timpson, a funded evening in the bar and the bosses out of the way.

What to do?

Make sure you have clear measures in place, both individually and for the work of the team. Apart from providing direction and joint understanding of the work to be done, it identifies the achievements to celebrate.

How long is it since you last had some form of celebration or get-together? If it is any longer than two months, sort out a date now for the near future. Make a note in your diary at regular intervals to ensure that you do not forget this important aspect of team life.

- Complete the Timpson test questionnaire (see Chapter 6) for all your team – if you score less than 70 out of 100, make time to find out more about your people.
- If you are shy or introverted, concentrate on the one-to-one elements and buddy up with an extrovert colleague or team member for the team events.
- If you have shy or introverted people in your team, find out if

> team members know what they enjoy or appreciate. You need to find a way of congratulating that will not be an embarrassment. A regular quiet 'Thank you' with minimal fuss may be the best way.
> - Allocate time to find out how the team want to celebrate. Consider giving them a budget and hand over responsibility for making the arrangements. Apart from the respect this shows, it is one way of getting them on board without encountering the British Eeyore tendency of looking for the flaw.
> - If your company does not have a budget for reward and recognition, suggest it to the senior leaders, pointing out the value of encouragement.
> - Say 'Thank you' whenever you can – it is a small effort with huge impact.
> - Always attend team gatherings and get your boss to join you, even if only for a short time. Remember: giving your time shows enormous respect and will be repaid tenfold in commitment.

Everyone wants to be appreciated – it is human nature to enjoy that moment of acclaim. However, look for the style that suits the culture, company and country. Remember the great company cry – match the actions to the people. With the appropriate method, recognition sends a number of messages – we appreciate a job well done, we are a company that looks for excellence and this is the best way to behave in the workplace. Even those who apparently brush it away will take the validation to heart.

Once begun, it is important not to backtrack – raising expectations is wonderful as long as you are prepared to keep going. Do not feel you have to do it all alone: make it a team responsibility and it will become even more of a pleasure.

Care between colleagues

Having friends at work is a significant element of a great workplace. This is part of what leads to comments about belonging and feeling like a family. It is a sad reflection on your business if people do not know each other well. You probably spend as much time with close colleagues as you do with your partner, so it is a terrible waste if you do not get on.

Part of the management task is to provide opportunities for these relationships to develop. Not constantly sitting on people's backs to stop them having a natter on Monday morning is one example. Treat people like grown-ups and they will behave like grown-ups, so enabling them to chat, trusting that they will get the work done, is important.

Many great relationships are forged when people negotiate difficult times together. We all remember those who rally round when times are tough, whether that means a project that is not going well or trouble with the kids or elderly parents. It is those human experiences that link us. We all have our moments, so it is comforting to see everyone pull together for someone. When our turn comes, we trust we shall receive the same level of care.

If this is modelled and encouraged by management, colleagues will pick it up. When friendships are made there is a natural inclination to help out, but unless this is shown to be acceptable in the workplace, colleagues will hesitate and wait until the boss has gone or the day ends. Enabling and encouraging that support when it is needed will pay dividends. Managers earn trust and commitment when they show their humanity in the face of need.

Finding the right balance between fun and focused work is tough. It is so easy to clamp down when the pressure is on, yet a short time of relaxation may renew the effort.

Service between people can exist only where there is trust in an organisation. Treating your team like grown-ups means trusting them to do a good job – why would they chat to the detriment of their company? It is tough to see laughter and chat when you know there is a lot to do, but you must take into account personal needs. Some people need regular breaks if they are to focus well on the work, and a lighthearted moment will spur them on to greater things. Equally, the chance to chat through a problem or concern with a colleague can make all the difference and focus the mind, so the burden of the task is halved.

The amount of chat and laughter in your team will depend almost entirely on what sort of manager you are. If you keep a tight rein on the work schedule, there will be little conversation on anything other than the task at hand. If you trust your people and believe they want to do the best job they can, you can turn a blind eye when a natural break is in progress – you may even lead it.

Action steps

- Experiment with allowing more chat than usual and see what happens. On the other hand, do this only if you are willing to keep an open mind and ensure that there will be no repercussions. If it does not work well, tell the team about your aspirations and concerns and see what they suggest. Remember you are dealing with grown-ups.
- Itemise the work to be done on a specific day. Identify a way to measure how effectively it has been done and assess the outputs.
- Then let go of the reins for a day and see what happens to the workload. Depending on your relationship to date, this may require you to go away or to stop for a chat yourself to show you are easy with the behaviour. At the end of the day, assess the workload using the same measures and see what the difference is.
- Ask for feedback from someone who will give you a straight answer. If the output is under par, ask for feedback on how you might be influencing it, plus ideas for how to allow people more freedom and trust without a loss to the work.
- Listen carefully to suggestions, and experiment with different forms of behaviour.
- Demonstrate your appreciation by celebrating and congratulating publicly when work is done well or when an effort has been made, even if the output was not successful.

That Bob Henry will stop his work to talk to anyone who needs his time is a fantastic example to the people of CORGI. There is no need to brave the posh office of the CEO, he is always available with a chair ready and waiting. This impacts on the way people behave towards each other, taking the time to listen when the need arises. Keith has worked with Bob for 12 years, and so knows the type of support given very well. One of the things he loves at CORGI is that 'Whenever you are on a black day, people give you loads of support, but they don't get in the hole with you.' An emphasis on listening and learning from experience ensures that people will unpick a problem in a positive way rather than joining a communal moan. Encourage this form of conversation and support all you can. It means that your people are learning from the daily round – the best education there is.

Service to the community

People with high levels of self-esteem have energy left over to help others, and great companies take advantage of this to support the community. This can mean supporting local schools and organisations, raising money for a specific charity, or acting on a wider scale for the good of other countries in the world.

There are numerous advantages to this, only one being community benefits. Painting the walls of a children's home with people from other teams is a great way of building relationships that will oil the wheels of business in the future. It develops pride in the company and understanding of how to sustain effort and work with new people, plus the opportunity to practise leadership.

Wragge & Co. offer their specific skills to community organisations, working in partnership with them on a no-fee basis. Lee, a legal executive, has an autistic son who regularly visits the office. While setting up a local branch of a charity that supports autistic families, Lee was given the support of a lawyer to cover the necessary legal work. The lawyer has now become a trustee who continues to help with business planning.

Team-building is another side-effect of serving the community. Shortly after Helen joined her team at Asda House the company undertook a sponsored walk. They raised £1,000, and she had the ideal opportunity to get to know people in a different way. Asda stores 'adopt' nearby schools and gain similar spin-off benefits – holding a Christmas party for local kids is no mean feat, requiring people to co-operate and work together if the children are to have a memorable experience. The results are highly effective teams, positive working relationships, great stories to tell and be proud of, and some tired but happy kids at the end of a long day.

Managers who listen carefully to their people will uncover all sorts of ideas for personal and community development. After Claire had been at CORGI for nine months, she ran an idea past Bob Henry. She had heard that local schools needed to find working people willing to talk about their experience of getting a job. Since she had started her working life with minimal qualifications and is now a successful accountant, she really wanted to encourage the kids to go for their dreams, even if it seemed hopeless just now.

There were huge benefits for Claire and CORGI in this project. It underlined all she had achieved which built self-esteem, and she used her leadership skills to take on the opportunity. It was not an easy audience to address and she was concerned they would be bored – but facing that fear and getting a positive outcome built confidence in her speaking ability. In fact, the children were genuinely interested in all she had to say, taking hope from her achievements. They also learned to look for the organisations that seek out talent regardless of entry qualifications – she is a fantastic advertisement for great companies!

Service to the customer

I make no apologies for putting this at the end of the chapter. Once you have the above factors in place, this is a natural follow-on. Provide people with the basics of customer service plus the company standards and they will be ready to do their very best job.

Think about it. When colleagues are proud of their company, they have a vested interest in maintaining excellent standards. They want to hold their heads high, without having to face negative stories. Bernard at Honda does not hesitate to tell people at a party that he works for Honda because he knows customers receive an excellent service. This is what everyone wants – to be able to speak proudly of their company without fear of a 'H'mm, yes, but I heard ...' response.

Container Store, number 1 in the US *Fortune* list for two years running, has an exceptionally strong reputation with customers. A businessman took an early flight out of his home town, forgetting the driving licence needed to hire a car. His wife was unsuccessful in getting the airline to carry it to him on the next flight, so she cast around desperately for inspiration. Approaching a woman standing in the queue, she asked her to take it to him. Given that it was clearly only a driving licence, she agreed, but asked why she had been chosen. 'You are wearing a Container Store T-shirt, so I knew you would help me.'

Stories like this enhance the reputation both in and out of the company. How proud must the Container Store colleague have felt to be so trusted, and how strong the story told by the woman to her friends. Going the extra mile is the stuff of exceptional PR and is most effective when told by someone with nothing to gain. When treated well, I become a loyal customer and great advocate – but this will not be achieved through standard practice alone. The ability to build a relationship is what really counts, and you cannot teach this, you can only model it.

When negative stories come to light through complaints, use it as a measure of how effectively your company is serving the colleague concerned. Find out how they are feeling about work and what help they need from you to do a better job.

People who care will seize the moment – but this requires them to feel cared for. Like Sonal at Flight Centre, who apologised to a disgruntled couple with a bunch of flowers and now books all their holidays for them. Go the extra mile for your people and trust them to do the same for your customers.

Summary

- Great company managers and leaders serve all the time – by listening, paying attention and supporting people to fulfil their true talents.
- Colleagues who are well cared for give great customer service. Make sure that you provide an environment of care, enhancing the well being of those who work with you, and your customer base will be equally healthy.
- Recognise good work and let everyone know what has happened – this will encourage more of the same.
- Encourage strong relationships throughout the company and treat people like adults. Then they will behave like adults with your customer.
- Serving the community is a positive gift to the world around you that engenders pride, loyalty and development in colleagues.

Ask customers for feedback

It takes a couple of years for poor customer service to hit the bottom line – get feedback and act on it consistently.

Customers talk about poor service – it is a way of dealing with the negative feelings. But by the time you realise that something is wrong, it is *really* wrong and hard to change.

Flight Centre realised the truth of this and decided to set up a customer service survey worldwide every six months – just what is it like to buy a holiday through a Flight Centre representative? Not much new there – but you would be amazed at how many organisations ask for feedback, collate it, study it and then put it away! At FC, detailed results are given to all managers, on the understanding that they need to work on the negatives that emerge. The upside is that it allows them to congratulate and reinforce the positives that make for exceptional service.

Companies have information coming out of their ears, and it is really tempting to gloss over yet another set of results when faced with countless meetings, e-mails and deadlines. 'Head stuck in the sand' can be appealing at times. Great companies really want to know how they are doing. As Gary Hogan says:

> We're always questioning ourselves, just because it's working now are we kidding ourselves that we're getting this right? We need to know why people call, what they get, what their perception was of the service.

They want the detail, rather than just asking if people had a good or bad service – that is too nebulous and cannot be acted upon.

This totally sensible response takes courage and determination because it means being ready to listen to what you did not get right. Especially if you have had 20 years of 20 to 30 per cent compound improvement, as FC has, why bother putting yourself through it? But the horrible truth is that no one gets it right all the time – we are only human, after all. The trick is to accept that and welcome the tough feedback as learning. If you do not, the chances are that the problems will creep up on you and cause much bigger problems in the long run.

Action steps

- Check when you last asked customers – internal or external – for feedback. Work out what you need to know, whom you need to ask, and clarify the questions that will evoke this information. If you are not the analytical type, join forces with an expert in this field to ensure that you are making the most of the opportunity.
- Inform those who need to know and get the backing to act on the information gathered.
- Listen fully to the feedback – better not to ask than to ask and not listen.
- Plan how you will utilise the information. Make sure that the right people are included.

- Develop a timeline for action, with regular meetings to report back on findings and changes.
- Celebrate successes, including everyone involved.

Corporate social responsibility (CSR)

Once primary needs are answered we begin to think more widely of the world about us. This leads increasingly to strong corporate social responsibility initiatives in organisations.

Wragge & Co. – serving the needs of Birmingham
Steve had been a solicitor with Wragge & Co. for a while and felt the need for a change. Because of his loyalty to the firm he gave his manager plenty of warning (always the sign of a great working relationship). He explained that he really enjoyed his work but wanted to be more useful, and so was thinking of working for a charity. Keen to hold on to a good person, but also knowing that the firm wanted to extend its work in the community, his manager sent Steve off to write a CSR job description.

He has been happily working in this capacity for some time now, doing everything from raising funds by swimming with sharks, sleeping rough alongside the senior partner, John Crabtree, to raise awareness for the plight of the homeless, and building strong partnership connections, to working on behalf of a number of charities in Birmingham. There is a great deal to do in this area and the firm is making an extremely positive contribution.

St Luke's – serving the needs of community and planet
Nina came to St Luke's from the Prince's Trust with no experience of advertising. Her role is twofold: to tend the culture of St Luke's and to enable the company to provide service to the outside world. The range of work done is extremely varied and, as you would expect, highly innovative.

The agency has what it calls 'social shares' – a virtual currency that enables it to provide help outside the confines of the business. Agency members began by striving to make St Luke's a carbon-neutral company. Having measured their negative environmental impact, they work in partnership with Future Forests, an organisation that offsets emissions through such projects as planting mango trees, which have an equal and opposite positive effect on carbon levels.

Time social shares enable

colleagues to use work time for social projects that touch their hearts. Financial social shares fund programmes such as the St Luke's Scholarship in partnership with YCTV, which sponsors young people to attend a media programme designed to give them a head start in the industry.

Nina manages all these initiatives and more. Given the freedom to extend her thinking and work in areas that are her passion, she can see a direct impact. Like the young woman who recently won a prize from YCTV and has been offered the chance to develop a career in TV – here is someone whose life would be much less interesting if it were not for the CSR work of St Luke's.

Asda – store of the community
Asda are highly active in supporting their communities. In October 2000 they launched their own standard of what makes for a socially responsible store. To qualify, stores demonstrate good relationships with their local communities including schools, charities, the emergency services, MPs and local suppliers. This is achieved both through fund-raising for charities and by people getting directly involved in issues that matter to them personally.

Helen Oates joined the finance team at Asda House in 2002 and was soon involved in a fashion show to raise funds for charity. Modelling George clothes, the team worked out their own choreography and music, attracting 200 people. Everyone pulled together and played their part, even Helen when she was asked to wear a nightie. 'It was a bit revealing – oh, my goodness! – but I managed to do it.'

But this is not all she has done. The team have adopted Broom Court, a home for handicapped children, and she has already spent considerable time there, painting murals, planting a seasonal garden and just getting to know the kids. There are benefits all round, not just to Broom Court. Helen has got to know her team really well – better than in previous workplaces – and she quite rightly feels a huge sense of pride in all they have achieved together.

Action steps

- Talk with your team to discover what community initiatives they are keen to undertake.
- If you can set about this on your own as a team, work out ways of achieving your desired end. Choose the people who will support you, and plan how you will celebrate your success. Make sure that necessary work time is set aside to support people in this activity.
- If you need company agreement, create a plan together and make a presentation to the relevant leaders. Involve the whole team and use the opportunity to build relationships with leaders in the company.
- Send out the call to others in the company who could be interested in working with you.
- If you want the company to do more, get together a group of interested people to prepare a proposal for a company-wide CSR programme. Look at the DTI website on Corporate Social Responsibility for information of what other companies are doing. Take it to the relevant leaders and advocate your case.

Chapter 11

Presenting a compelling case for action: bringing people on board

If you have read this far, you know a lot about what great companies do. You also have plenty of ideas which you have hopefully tried for yourself and are beginning to see some results from your endeavours. And this in turn will inspire you to keep going.

But to garner the positive results described in Chapter 1 you need others to join in. So now is the time to begin using your influence with your manager or your senior team. The first task is to convince them that this is not just a touchy-feely 'nice to have' but that it is also about making money. The second is to convince others that work-life can be better than it is presently, that it must get better for the sake of the business, and that you are committed to creating change.

Organisations are made up of people, and people are always resistant to change. Some resist for 10 seconds then get on with it, others can hold out for a really long time. You have to persuade them this is for the best and encourage them to take on – or even relish – the challenges.

Depending on the type of culture you have already, you will be pushing uphill or on an open door. The first part of this chapter looks at how to proceed when the senior team are open to suggestion and the second half suggests what you can do if you are on your own.

Regardless of what actions you decide to take, your own behaviour is a powerful tool for promoting change. Do not talk one way and behave in another. From this moment on, be a great company manager. Identify your principles, understand the behaviours that demonstrate them and let that guide your actions. When you fail, acknowledge it, take the learning and begin again. If you are consistent in your valuing of people, you will make an impact.

There are many ways to take the first steps:

- approach the senior team
- invite the HR department to act as enabler of the great company culture
- build critical mass from your present position
- work with your own team
- plough a lone furrow.

Approaching the senior team

If your organisation is already on the way to great company culture, your senior team will be ready to listen. So go direct to the top if you can – it will make the job much easier. Leaders who are behind the process will have the greatest success in setting principles, vision and direction. Get them on board and behaving in great company style and you are well on your way.

Give them this book to read, give them a copy of the *Sunday Times 100 Best Companies to Work For* list and point out the graph that shows great company performance against the FTSE All Share (Appendix 3, slide 3). You may suggest entering for the list yourselves – it is a great way to benchmark. Above all, share your enthusiasm – if you are really excited by the ideas and prospects of a great culture and can see specifically how it will fit the company, this will be your most influential tool.

Remember, the measure of a great company is how colleagues feel about coming to work each day. The effectiveness of the business comes entirely from their enthusiasm about the work, so finding out about the present reality is the obvious starting point. A diagnostic process will offer some profound information – whether new discoveries or different ways of looking at what is already known. The usual path is to track the business figures and results carefully, letting people issues take second place. Great company culture demands that people issues come up to the same level of importance, because it is people who fuel the numbers and profit.

Building a convincing business case is essential if you are to bring senior leaders with you. Use the evidence here to explain how great company culture will impact directly on the business.

Suggested elements are:

- the company context
- issues that presently tax your leaders
- the present culture and its impact on the bottom line
- identifying great company competitors
- suggestions for next steps
- a call to action.

The company context

You need to set the scene, and in doing so, share your passion for the subject. Look for a way to summarise in a few words the main reasons for suggesting great company culture. This may be:

- a statement about your place in the market
- the vision, and how well you are on track – or not
- a statement that summarises how people feel about the organisation.

An example might be to put up three statements along the lines of:

Positive: We manage to hit our targets financially.
Issue: People do not stay here over the long term.
Question: How much better could we do if people enjoyed working here?

Alternatively, you might use a direct quote from a colleague that summarises how many people feel about the workplace. As long as the original speaker cannot be identified or 'dropped in it', put this up and let it speak for itself.

Remember to behave in great company style from the outset. Use your integrity and be fair and honest. You need to connect to the heart as well as the mind. So show how strongly you feel about your subject and invite the senior team on a journey of discovery.

Issues that presently tax your leaders

Collate the issues that are of greatest concern at the time of presentation and show how they connect to the need for a great culture. Give as many figures as you can to build your case.

Possible issues are:

Recruitment costs
Find out how much the company spends each year on recruiting the

right people. To indicate how effective this process is, align with the retention figures.

Retention figures

Show how much it costs the company each time an employee chooses to leave. Recruiting takes time and money, but this is often the least of it. Once the decision is made, attention is already divided as the departing person works out how to hand over and aligns to the forthcoming challenge. The incoming person has to get up to speed with the work, colleagues, customers, and the team, and adjust life to the new demands. We are talking about a good six months before life is anywhere near normal for those on the receiving end.

Find out the annual colleague retention figures, including when most people leave – ie is it in the first six months, or are you losing your experienced people? Identify the cost in terms of loss of time, expertise and experience. You may be able to get this from your HR department if it is a statistic they track. If not, talk with your peers to find out what has been happening in their areas. Ensure that they know why you want the information, and make sure you do not identify a particular department, if it will cause difficulties.

Succession

Talk about the effectiveness of succession. Is the company developing leaders/managers for the future? Are the leaders on the board passing on their expertise to those who will follow? External appointments to the senior team may advocate bringing in new blood. Put it to them that relevant expertise and company experience is lost when people leave to further their career, so there is value in growing internal leaders. The concern about needing fresh thinking can be answered by the next point.

Career development

See if HR can give you statistics about career development. For example: how many high potential colleagues are getting experience in different parts of the business (thereby also bringing fresh thinking to the new area)? How many internal mentors are passing on their knowledge and experience? How often are appraisals taking place, and how many people have personal development plans (PDPs)? How many people have coaches? Find out if people believe they can develop their career in the company. Ask if they are getting the training and development they need to do their work well.

Absenteeism

Find out what level of absenteeism you have in the company. You can judge this from your direct experience with your own people or speak to HR to see if it is something they measure. If people are taking a lot of time out in odd days, it may be due to a lack of engagement in their work. You do not want sick people coming in to work, but those who 'throw a sickie' can take a sizable chunk off the bottom line. This makes it worth addressing the reasons why they are not fully connected and committed to the business.

Diversity

Study the diversity profile. Does the organisation appeal to a range of people who can bring new ideas and angles into the business? Are you making the most of the value of age and experience?

Customer service

Look at customer satisfaction figures, if they are available. How effective is the service given to internal and external customers? Do colleagues build strong relationships with customers? Does the company evoke a strong level of customer commitment? If there are no figures available, do a spot-check with internal customers – start with your own and find out how satisfied they are with the service you provide.

The present culture and its impact on the bottom line

Use some direct examples of what the great companies do and how they relate to those who work for them – there are plenty of stories you can use from this book. Choose those that relate to work in your own organisation and draw a direct comparison where possible.

Then put up the graph reproduced in the *Sunday Times* of the quoted company results set against the FTSE All Share and use any of the statistics quoted in this book to show the impact of effective people management on day-to-day business. I have set out a draft PowerPoint presentation for you to refer to, containing relevant hard data and including this graph – see Appendix 3.

Identifying great company competitors

Depending on the industry sector, it may be useful to list the names of your competitors who appear on the list. As soon as the list comes out, the named companies see a jump in recruitment requests, bringing high-calibre people into view. The supplement is an obvious place for young hopefuls to look when they want to move jobs – why work in a place that offers little fun, development or future, when you can work for one of the greats? So if a competitor is named, they will have the pick of the talent pool, leaving you to make do with the under-qualified, unmotivated minnows!

Suggestions for next steps

If you are not sure of the best way to begin, I suggest one of the following:

A *diagnostic process*

Find out exactly what the culture is like at present. When you arrive new to a workplace, you see habits and unspoken traditions that surprise or delight you, but your awareness becomes dulled as you settle in and begin doing things in the same way as everyone else. For this reason, consider using outside consultants, preferably those who have not worked with you recently, but who have worked with great companies and can bring their ideas and experience to the process. Experience shows that someone with an external perspective can give good feedback in a short space of time with clear suggestions for next steps.

Undertake a company survey

Most organisations undertake colleague surveys at regular intervals and it is an excellent way to stay up to date with the working experience. Consider using the *100 Best Companies to Work For* methodology. The advantage of this is that all questions specifically target the capabilities and characteristics that mark out great companies. Furthermore, the results can be benchmarked against the *100 Best*. This gives a very clear indication of how close the company is to being great and the areas that need to be addressed to fill the gaps.

Apply to be added to the Best Companies list

If you think your company is doing well enough to get on the list, put in an application. If the company does not make the grade, there will be no public mention of the application, so it is not a PR risk. However, you will receive a summary of results and can access more in-depth results which will give you an idea of what your company can do to improve.

Or when there is an obvious starting place:

Improvements and piloting

You may be able to identify specific elements of the culture that are not functioning in great company style – for example, the communication systems. Alternatively, you may have leaders/managers who are keen to make changes in their specific area and would like to be a pilot for the whole company.

Put forward suggestions for next steps with the short- and long-term benefits of each:

Leader contact

A really simple first step is to remind leaders about the power of a 'Thank you' and about taking the time to talk with people they pass in the office. Becoming a leader changes how people see you – even though you feel the same now as you always did. Those casual comments about the football or the kids are worth their weight in gold to people on the receiving end.

Developing great company managers

Managers are the glue of great company culture. It makes sense therefore to inculcate a great company mindset at this level – it is one of the fastest ways to promote a great culture. It will improve communication, increase the effectiveness of the appraisal process, ensure that succession is consistently high on the agenda, build celebration and reward into the system, and create strong teams with a sense of pride in their achievements.

Leadership development

Leaders have a significant role to play. They set the tone, convey vision and principles, role model the required behaviours and create the environment in which people can thrive. Enabling leaders to develop their emotional intelligence and understanding of what makes people tick will make them more effective as 'keepers of the culture'.

Involving colleagues in building the great company culture

Each company has its own signature of greatness determined by what colleagues want from their work, so involve them in deciding what will make each day great. Ask them for ideas for change. Use every working experience as a test-bed, providing information for other parts of the business. Invite people to run each piece of work 'great-company-style'. Gather ideas regularly on a formal basis, offering people the chance to talk through what worked well and what did not work at all. Celebrate success and spread the news of what is going well in the company newsletter, on the intranet or just via team meetings and the grapevine. Have regular open forums and invite colleagues to join a discussion on the great company culture. Bring in respected people champions to provide support and empower people to act on ideas that receive acclaim.

The call to action

Use a great company quote, statistic or colleague comment to inspire the leaders to action. Remember: great company culture is emotional – it is what inspires the heart, builds connections, and engenders pride. Logic wins minds, and you have offered that in results and statistics earlier in the presentation. Leave on a note that inspires the heart.

The HR department as enabler of great company culture

Companies and organisations are always working on training and development in some part of the business. Each initiative can be approached in a great company manner so that ideas are embedded through every person who undertakes a programme, coaching or training.

People departments – or human resource departments, as they are generally called – have a huge role to play in supporting the company in building a strong culture. Taking the great company philosophy and making it the context for people development changes not only what you do but how you do it. Look at issues of development in that light and emotional intelligence becomes the underpinning for managers and leaders, emphasising understanding self and others, listening skills, coaching, and inspiration.

HR is also in a position to further the culture by recalling the stories and building them into induction, so that everyone knows the history and overall context of the company. In Southwest Airlines, the head of HR is known as the 'Keeper of the Culture', heading up a team of storytellers who keep the history of the company alive. Knowing where we come from is essential for companies as well as for people – it is one way we understand ourselves.

However, this does not mean that HR can take full responsibility for creating a great culture. The line management must retain ownership of the initiative if it is to work, even though some line managers would love to hand it over in full! Everyone must play their part, working collaboratively to ensure getting the very best out of every contribution. And without managers taking their rightful place at the centre of their own team culture, there is no chance of developing a positive workplace (see Chapter 6).

To assess how effectively HR is supporting the line, consider present training and development initiatives with a great company eye:

- Begin with the guiding principles of the company – how well are they reflected in the development work you do to date?
- Consider the programmes and initiatives you have in place and see how they contribute to or detract from a great company culture.
- How well does your leadership development support a positive people culture? Is it evenly spread between business understanding and people skills? Include the elements of *great company culture* and *servant leadership* in the process to encourage them to take a lead.
- Managers are really important in great company culture – how much support do they get with their people skills? They ensure the development of talent, and measure and reward effectiveness – without them, people are working in isolation. At Flight Centre, everyone is considered to be a leader and the team leaders are the most important people in the company – do you value your managers this highly?
- Great company culture is a very real way for HR to impact on the bottom line. It is an opportunity to move out of the rather negative mindset some companies hold, and into a positive, strategic role. Create a presentation that will reframe HR in the minds of the senior leaders, using statistics and stories from this book.

- Evaluate the present recruitment process against the information in this book. Consider how closely the process relates to the principles – are you getting the people who will feel at home with the organisation? Balance this against the length of time people stay – this is a good indicator of effective recruitment.
- Look at reward and recognition – being valued and appreciated is something we all want. It is the route to high performance. People want to do a good job and be recognised for it. We are not just talking about money here. Congratulations, expressions of appreciation at a team meeting, a quiet word to say 'Thank you and well done,' a cake or glass of champagne on someone's birthday are all ways of recognising someone's efforts.
- Above all, make sure you are a 'great' team – role modelling is the most effective way forward. If you say one thing and do another, your initiative will be dead in the water. To quote Stephen Covey, 'You cannot talk your way out of something you have behaved your way into.'

Building critical mass from your present position

It is not always possible to begin at the top. You may not have a role that gives you the direct access, or the leaders may not be open to persuasion or believe that culture really makes a difference. If this is the case in your workplace, be on the lookout for supporters. Once enough people are on board, the impact will become evident. There is nothing more persuasive than seeing a team doing really well. The wise leader will want to know what is happening, and then you have first-hand evidence that how people feel makes a difference to the business.

Choose your battles carefully. Find people who are strong advocates: talk with them about great company culture and your own feelings/concerns about the working environment. Invite them to join you in creating change. Work out a plan of action together, built around testing your perceptions, changing behaviour and recording results. Do this by:

- gathering information
- developing an action plan
- feeding back results to the relevant people.

Gather information

Individually test out your perceptions and assumptions. Find out whether other people feel as you do, whether they are happy at work or cannot wait to get out of the door at night.

There are a number of ways to gather information:

- Seek out one or two of those people in the company who have great networks and know what everyone is doing. They can be fantastic at gathering feedback. Ask them about the 'word on the street'.
- Talk to your peers and ask about their experience of the company. Do they feel positive, excited and enthusiastic about work? Find out if they would recommend their best friend to apply for a job – this is a good measure of feeling.
- Get your advocates to speak to their teams and find out how they feel about work. However, this will work only where you have a culture in which openness and honesty already exist to a certain extent. If people are unwilling to tell their manager the truth, you will get back only what they think you want to hear. If this is the case, and you have access to a budget, bring in an independent external person who can have the conversations for you while also protecting anonymity.
- Engage in conversation in an informal way to find out how people feel. Be prepared to talk about your own experience to see if that resonates. Share your excitement about the alternatives.

Make it clear that you will hold personal details in confidence and that there will be no repercussions. Then make sure everyone concurs with this. If you let people down now, they will never tell you the truth again.

Develop an action plan

Meet with your advocates and share information. Look for the common themes and identify ways to address them. Make agreements about action in your own spheres of influence and share progress at regular intervals.

You may have to change your own behaviour and mindsets quite markedly. Just because you care about the changes does not mean that they will be easy to make. Supporting each other will be of paramount importance – and do not forget to celebrate success, however small.

Feed back results

When results begin to emerge, work out whom you need to talk to. Now is your chance to advocate on a wider basis. Gather your 'team' of change agents and present the work you have done, the experiences you have been through, and the outputs achieved. Be clear about what has worked well and what has not worked, about the learning you have taken in, and about suggestions on how to take your initiative to the next stage.

You may be able to engage a senior sponsor through your network. If you can arrange a meeting, be ready with an 'elevator speech', getting your point across in one minute. You want to make the most of your chance and you also never know when you might bump into someone who could help your cause. Feel free to use it on other people you meet – take every opportunity to spread the word.

Working with your own team

Even if there is no interest from others in the company, do not give up. You can act now with your own team and begin to create a great team culture.

You need to find out how people are experiencing work-life at present. Before you begin the conversations, make sure that you are willing to act on what you hear. If colleagues are making requests in relation to something you cannot influence eg pay scales – be clear about it and pass the information on to the relevant people. When you do have influence, be sure to act – or explain why you are not doing so – or you will be further back than you are now. A prime feature of great company culture is 'walking the talk' – and if you express an interest but do nothing, you will create a sense of disillusionment that will cost you in the long term.

When you are ready to, bring your team together and talk with them about their life at work. The emphasis needs to be on your ears – listen carefully, ask questions to make sure you understand exactly what is being said, including their ideas for action. You do not have to do this all alone – that is the point. You create the great team culture with them, not for them.

Remember: your job is to create an environment in which they can do their best work – your most frequent question must be 'What can I do to help you?'

Keep a diary of what happens, so that you can talk other people through it when they ask what you are doing differently.

Ploughing a lone furrow

If you do not have a team, you still do not need to give up. Individual people can have a profound effect on an organisation, if they are willing to spend the time and the energy. This is a great example of your bread cast upon the water coming back as a ham sandwich (see the John Crabtree story at the end of Chapter 2). Behaving in great company style with everyone you encounter through the day will have an impact on the workplace. Act as a networker, introducing people who have common interests, whether at work or home; be interested in how people are – make them feel valued; congratulate when you hear about achievements. You will make a difference, and it will help you move forward in your career because you will be seen as a positive force in the company.

Since it can be hard to keep up your enthusiasm alone, take every opportunity to talk with like-minded people. Depending on the size of your organisation, you may already know where your 'soul-mates' are. If not, perhaps you can write something for the company magazine about the list and see who responds. Ask about for people who have the same ideas about management, or go outside to conferences or seminars to top up your ideas and enthusiasm.

If your work environment is so negative that you fear a punitive response to any of the above actions, it may be time to look for another job. Weigh up the pros and cons and decide whether the cost is too high if you stay or if you leave. This may be a good time to look for one of the great companies and take your energy where it will be appreciated. Or it may be that life holds enough challenge at present and you ought to stay put. Be honest and take care of yourself in the best way possible. Just remember that there are options out there for a really exciting place to work, when you are ready for it.

Summary

- People are your competitive advantage. Everything else you do can be copied. Maximising your people makes sense on all fronts.
- To effect change, look first to your own behaviour. It is pointless to

advocate to others when you are not acting in great company style yourself. Be a positive role model.

- The most straightforward approach is to the senior team. They make a major impact on company culture, so bring them on board if you can. Present them with the facts general to great companies and specific to your company, and suggest positive next steps.
- The HR function can be a great advocate with the ability to make a strong impact. Align all HR actions to great company culture, including your own teamworking.
- As a manager, begin to build critical mass. Find like-minded colleagues and look to your way of working. Agree actions for change and keep track of the results. When people comment, tell them what you have done.
- If you are a lone voice, work with your own team. Create a great workplace together and show how much difference it makes. Give each other support to continue and celebrate your successes.
- As an individual, behave in great company style and you will be a catalyst to others. Network, support and celebrate − by the model you present you can create change.

Appendix 1: Useful information

The Sunday Times 100 Best Companies To Work For list

To access a list of the Best Companies to Work For look on the website www.sunday-times.co.uk

If you think your company is great, you may want to consider putting in an application to be added to the list, which is produced by Best Companies Ltd.

There are two options:

- If you have between 50 and 249 employees in the company, you can apply to the *Best Small to Medium Companies to Work For* list.
- If you have over 250 employees, you can apply to the *100 Best Companies to Work For* list.

The application process

Step 1

Nominate your company via the Best Companies website www.best-companies.co.uk

Step 2

A random group of employees are surveyed, using the Best Companies™ Employee Survey, to find out what they think of the company. Topics include leadership in the company, respect for the individual, opportunities for development, pay and benefits, and the overall environment.

Step 3

Participating companies are asked to complete the Best Companies™ Questionnaire. This gives you the opportunity to highlight what you think makes you one of the best.

Step 4

A proportion of the companies receive a workplace visit from one of the Best Companies researchers to see at first hand what the company looks and feels like.

Step 5

Final selections are made and the list is published.

To access a copy of the most recent list supplement, access the DTI listing below.

The Best Companies Employee Survey

You can also use the Best Companies™ Employee Survey as a measure of internal colleague satisfaction. This has three specific benefits:

- The questions are designed specifically to explore the issues of great company culture.
- It will show you exactly which areas to target to get the most change in the culture.
- You can measure your own company against the *100 Best Companies*.

To find out more, contact Best Companies on their website or telephone 01978 856222.

The Department of Trade and Industry

The DTI has a number of interesting things on offer:

Living Innovation

This research studied innovation in UK companies and culminated in a very useful report, plus a survey you can use to measure levels of innovation in your own company.

You can access and use the questionnaire directly on line via www.lidiagnostic.com or www.innovation.gov.uk

For case studies of what other companies have done see www.livinginnovation.org or www.innovation.gov.uk

To read the report, write to DTI Admail 528, London SW1W 8YT, or telephone 08701 502500, or fax 08701 502333.

The Sunday Times 100 Best Companies To Work For list

If you would like a smart copy to use as part of a presentation to your leaders/colleagues, contact the DTI via the numbers or address listed above and they will send one to you.

Other DTI publications

There are a large number of helpful publications that you can read about and access via the addresses/numbers above. Alternatively, visit the main DTI website at www.dti.gov.uk . Two examples are:

- *Innovation Review*, a report of the work DTI does to support innovation in UK companies.

- *Scoreboards*, information that enables you to benchmark against other companies on research and development expenditure and value added. This provides a useful addition to the information in the PowerPoint presentation in Appendix 3.

The Chamber of Commerce

Your local Chamber of Commerce will have networking events that include interesting speakers. This is one way to stay up to date with the latest thinking and new ideas while building interesting contacts.

Visit their website www.chamberonline.co.uk for your local branch.

Information about the best companies

If you want information about specific sectors or companies to support your case to management, visit the website www.sunday-times.co.uk On the left-hand side of the screen is a list which includes the *Best Companies to Work For*. This will take you direct to the list.

Click on any company and you will see information of size, turnover, staff turnover, etc.

Related books

I read the following and they all taught me something about the issues discussed in this book:

James Autry, *Love and Profit*
A heart-warming book, full of good ideas and permission/encouragement to act in the right way.

Margaret Wheatley, *Leadership and the New Science*
An explanation of quantum physics in relation to management.

Kevin and Jackie Freiburg, *Nuts*
The story of Southwest Airlines.

Robert Levering, *A Great Place to Work*
Robert developed the methodology that evaluates the Best Companies list for *Fortune* magazine and the *Financial Times*.

Daniel Goleman, *The New Leaders*
Leadership and emotional intelligence.

Ricardo Semler, *The Seven-Day Weekend*
An example of turning traditional work ethics on their head to develop an interesting and highly successful business.

Jim Collins, *Good to Great*
A fascinating study of what separates those companies that grow strong from troubled times and those that fail.

John Timpson, *The Complete Guide to Upside-Down Management*
John's very practical view of what I would call 'servant leadership'.

Jeffrey Pfeffer, *The Human Equation*
This is full of useful information and statistics about the impact of great company culture on the business. It is mostly based on manufacturing in the USA.

James Autry, *The Servant Leader*
A really useful view of servant leadership from a true advocate.

Julian Richer, *The Richer Way*
Teachings from an entrepreneur who built a strong and effective great culture.

David Maister, *Practice What You Preach*
A source of useful statistics and examples from the USA to influence those who still need convincing.

James M. Kouzes and Barry Z. Posner, *The Leadership Challenge*
An interesting study and model of leadership that sets out to engage the heart.

Steve Hilton and Giles Gibbons, *Good Business*
A study of Corporate Social Responsibility and how business can be a positive force for good in the world.

David Stauffer, *Business the Cisco Way*
The story of how Cisco Systems developed.

Richard Reeves, *Happy Mondays*
Changing our attitudes to work and owning up to the pleasure it can bring.

Matt Weinstein, *Managing to Have Fun*
Full of ideas for having fun, enhancing colleague satisfaction and finding personal pride in work.

Marvin Weisbord, *Productive Workplaces*
An interesting read on management theories, how they impact the workplace, what we can take forward, and how to create the change we need.

Barry J. Gibbons, *Dream Merchants and Howboys*
Fun account of entrepreneurs – or nutters, as he calls them. Includes Herb Kelleher (founder and ex-leader of Southwest Airlines), Steve Jobs and Anita Roddick, amongst others.

William Byham, *Zapp! The Lightning of Empowerment: How to improve productivity, quality and employee satisfaction*
Great company culture told in a story. It makes an easy read for busy managers, with good ideas along the way.

Appendix 2:
Company profiles

The following companies have been researched for this book. For you to find the best comparison for your own organisation, I have included some basic statistics about each company. Further information can be found via their specific websites.

MICROSOFT's computer software and business solutions help businesses realise their potential, and through its vision empowers people through great software any time, anywhere and on any device. Microsoft is recognised as the employer of choice in the IT sector, and was voted number 1 in the *Sunday Times Best Companies to Work For* 2003 survey. In the UK there are 1,605 employees who produce annual sales of $32,187 million globally.

RICHER SOUNDS is Britain's largest hi-fi and home cinema retailer. Founded in 1978 by Julian Richer, it has 450 colleagues and an annual turnover of £100 million from 47 stores. It was named as the second-best company to work for in the UK in 2003. David Robinson is the CEO.

FLIGHT CENTRE is part of a global travel business and has been in the UK since 1995. It has 80 shops with 352 colleagues and annual sales of £100 million. The company was number 3 in the *Sunday Times 100 Best Companies to Work For* list, number 6 in the *Financial Times Great Workplaces UK* list and in the *TOP 100 Great Workplaces EU* in 2003. Gary ('Boxer') Hogan is the CEO.

BROMFORD HOUSING GROUP was formed in 1963, and is a group of housing organisations, owning, managing and developing rented, shared ownership and other homes. They have more than 14,000 homes in management and are dedicated to the provision of affordable housing and associated care and support services. They have 520 colleagues and were number 5 in the *Sunday Times Best 100 Companies to Work For* list in 2003. Mick Kent is the CEO, Liz Walford is the operations director.

TIMPSON is a service retailer with 2,700 employees in over 750 branches and annual sales of £110 million. They were named as number 6 in the *Sunday Times 100 Best Companies to Work For* in 2003. John Timpson is the Chairman and CEO, James Timpson is the managing director.

ASDA is one of the biggest supermarkets chains in the UK. It has 265 stores, plus two stand-alone George Stores. There are 137,541 colleagues and annual sales have reached £13.2 billion. It is part of the Wal-Mart family and was voted number 1 in the *Sunday Times 100 Best Companies to Work For* list in 2002 and number 7 in 2003. Tony DeNunzio is the CEO, David Smith is the HR director.

HISCOX PLC is a specialist insurance group operating both inside and outside Lloyd's. It has 430 employees, is listed on the London Stock Exchange with a market capitalisation of approximately £450 million, and is a member of the FTSE 250.

The Group provides insurance and reinsurance at Lloyd's for large complex risks. Outside Lloyd's, its business in the UK and Europe provides insurance cover for business and professional customers through to high-value content insurance for high-net-worth individuals. Hiscox was named as the *Sunday Times'* tenth *Best Company to Work For* in the UK in 2003. Robert Hiscox is the Chairman, Bronek Masojada is the Group CEO.

HONDA (UK) is a subsidiary of Honda Motor Europe Ltd and was founded in 1965. The global company is the largest manufacturer of motorcycles and engines, and the seventh largest producer of cars in the world. Honda (UK) has annual sales in excess of £1 billion and employs over 350 Associates (employees). It was named as number 18 in the *Sunday Times 100 Best Companies to Work For* list in 2003.

A further 4,000 Associates are employed in the UK to work at Honda's manufacturing plants in Swindon. Mark Davies is the general manager of the motorcycle business, Ken Keir is the European managing director.

ASTRAZENECA is a major international health care business engaged in the research, development, manufacture and marketing of prescription pharmaceuticals and the supply of health care services. It is one of the top five pharmaceutical companies in the world, with health care sales of over $17.8 billion and leading positions in sales of gastrointestinal, oncology, cardiovascular, neuroscience and respiratory products. AstraZeneca is listed in the Dow-Jones Sustainability Index (global and European) as well as the FTSE4Good Index. The company was placed at number 21 in the *Financial Times* list of *50 Best Workplaces in the UK* in 2003.

WRAGGE & CO. LLP is a major UK law firm providing a full range of legal services for businesses worldwide. At the start of the 1990s the firm employed 321 people with 29 partners and had a turnover of £11 million. By 2003 it had grown to 108 partners, 1,100 people, and had a turnover of £77.8 million. Wragge & Co. LLP was listed at 34 in the *Sunday Times 100 Best Companies to Work For* list in 2003. John Crabtree was the senior partner (but has now retired from this post).

KENT MESSENGER GROUP is a family-owned media company which is passionate about serving the people of Kent. It publishes 18 local news-papers (including the UK's biggest-selling weekly newspaper, *Kent Messenger*), has five local radio stations (branded KM-fm), runs Kentonline.co.uk the local news website, produces monthly magazines and offers contract printing services.

Locally, the company is known as the 'KM' and the 760 colleagues work hard to strengthen the company's position as Kent's leading local media company by providing the best quality media. Annual turnover is £44 million. KM was listed at no 92 in the *Sunday Times 100 Best Companies to Work For* list in 2003

ST LUKE'S is a London advertising agency with 80 share-holder/employees. Named as UK Agency of the Year in 1997 St Luke's creates advertising for clients such as British Telecommunications plc, Clarks Shoes and The UK Government. In 2003 the agency was awarded The City of London Dragon Award for Corporate Social Responsibility.

CORGI is the national watchdog for gas safety in the United Kingdom, providing registration for all gas installers. The company has 287 col-leagues, with an annual turnover of £17.5 million. It registers, moni-tors and provides technical advice for approximately 44,000 gas businesses and about 94,000 individual gas operatives. It provides information services for the general public on matters relating to gas safety and investigates complaints against gas installing businesses. Bob Henry was the CEO until his recent retirement.

TD INDUSTRIES is a lifecycle provider of mechanical and electrical construction, facility management and service. With more than 1,350 partners (employees) they have an annual turnover of $240 million. TD has been in the *Fortune* magazine list of the *Best Companies to Work For* in the US since 1998 – being named consistently in the top ten throughout. Jack Lowe, Junior, is the CEO.

Appendix 3: PowerPoint slides

Evidence for the business case – a company presentation

How to use this presentation

This presentation is given as a guide only, to use at your discretion.

- Consider the specific issues that face your organisation and select the information that will support you in presenting the best case for action.

- I have put together some ideas on how to set out information about your own company – again as a guide. No one knows your company the way you do, so read this with the knowledge in mind and trust your judgement.

- Remember the great company culture connects to heart as well as mind. Take into consideration the emotional elements in your present company culture and find ways to speak to those.

- Most important of all – your behaviour and demeanour will have greatest impact on those you speak to. This presentation must a be strong reflection of what you believe, and should represent what you think is most important for the company. If you present with passion as well as calm rationale, you will have most chance of creating followers for your concerns.

Slide 1

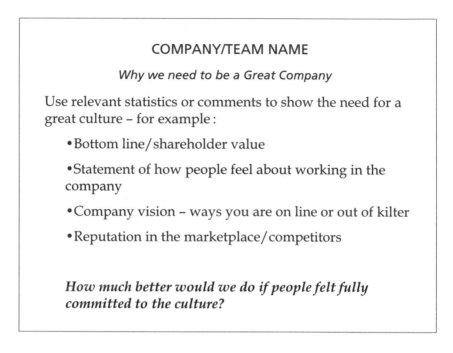

COMPANY/TEAM NAME

Why we need to be a Great Company

Use relevant statistics or comments to show the need for a great culture – for example:

- Bottom line/shareholder value

- Statement of how people feel about working in the company

- Company vision – ways you are on line or out of kilter

- Reputation in the marketplace/competitors

How much better would we do if people felt fully committed to the culture?

Commentary for slide 1

The purpose of this slide is to make a straight statement about the present reality and set the context for your input on the company culture.

- Sit back and take a long hard look at the present state of your team/company. How effective is the business?

- Always balance your comment between what is going well and what isn't – every organisation or team has its good points and it is important to acknowledge these. After all, if you are advocating being a great company, you have to start right now with appropriate behaviour and that means celebrating success and valuing effort.

Slide 2

COMPANY PERFORMANCE

If the information is available to you, show the most recent results from your company.

Follow this with the next slide, showing the performance of the *100 Best Companies to Work For.*

Commentary for slide 2

If you want to align senior leaders to your cause, it is important to show sound business reasons for developing a great company culture.

Evidence from the *Sunday Times* list shows that great companies outperform the FTSE All Share, which is a very compelling argument. In my experience, if you put this slide up first, you will have their attention for the 'softer' elements of the process.

If you believe your company could do better and you have access to the results, you could set the two alongside which will increase the power of your argument.

Slide 3

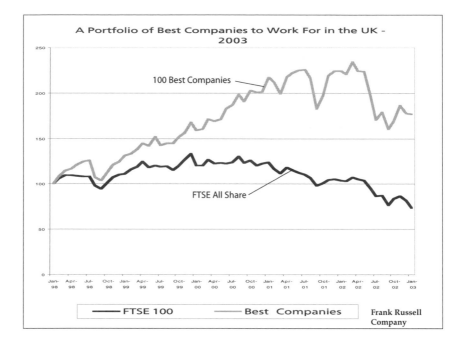

Commentary for slide 3

This graph shows the results of the quoted companies from the *Sunday Times 100 Best Companies to Work For* list 2003, produced by the Frank Russell Company.

Great company culture makes sense from a business perspective. People working to their potential are a major asset. After all, a business is just people working together – if you provide the environment that supports them to do their best work, the organisation will thrive.

Slide 4

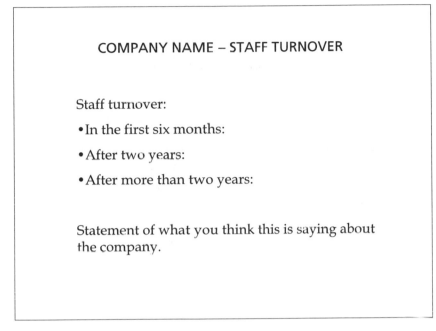

COMPANY NAME – STAFF TURNOVER

Staff turnover:

- In the first six months:

- After two years:

- After more than two years:

Statement of what you think this is saying about
the company.

Commentary for slide 4

Staff turnover is a significant measure of how strongly people feel about
a workplace. Talk with your HR department or use the figures from
your own part of the business to build a case for action. If you are regularly losing people – and particularly those who have been in the
company for a while - this may be a sign that all is not well with your
culture. It is certainly something to look at, given that recruitment costs
up to twice annual salary.

The main point is that on-going recruitment cost the company ina
number of ways:

- money and time - to recruit new people
- loss of expertise to company, that may go to competitors
- loss of customer relationships

One other factor to take into account when considering staff turnover is
the level of employee engagement. There are companies that have a very
low turnover rate because people have become demoralised and don't
believe they don't enjoy.

Slide 5

STAFF TURNOVER RATES

HISCOX (Insurance)	10%
FLIGHT CENTRE (Travel)	20%
ASDA (Retail)	27%
BROMFORD (Housing Association)	9%
WRAGGE & CO. (Legal)	17%
KENT MESSENGER (Publishing)	20%
HONDA (Manufacturing)	11%

Commentary for slide 5

These turnover rates are extremely good. The variables are to do with industry sector. For example travel is usually very high, a good 10 to 15% above Flight Centre. Retail and publishing are also normally high.

It has not been possible to find reliable industry averages. Choose the company closest to your own business and compare that to your own turnover rate. Alternatively, look in the latest *Sunday Times* list which gives turnover rates for all the companies in the list. For information on how to access this, look in Appendix Two.

Slide 6

> ### TRUST IN YOUR TEAM/COMPANY
>
> Describe your own sense of the levels of trust in the company or team you work in.
>
> Ask other people what they think – making sure that no one is identifiable in your feedback. Use some direct statements if you can.
>
> Use examples in the workings of the company that demonstrate high or low trust.
>
> Follow with the next slide on the cost of low-trust cultures.

Commentary for slide 6

If you believe you are in a low trust culture, be very careful how you address this. Make sure you act with integrity – people need to see that you are trustworthy. Assume that anything you say will cause waves and make sure you are not going to 'drop anyone in it'.

To determine whether you are in an appropriate person to address this issue in a such a presentation, think honestly about your own behaviour – how trustworthy have you been in the past? Check your perception with a colleague/friend who will be honest. If the response is positive, there is a chance your view will be respected.

If the answer is negative, consider whether you are willing to be open about it. If so, the best way forward is probably to acknowledge that you are not the ideal advocate, but that you want to improve and would like the company to join you in making the change.

If you are not willing to change, then great company culture is not the way forward for you.

Slide 7

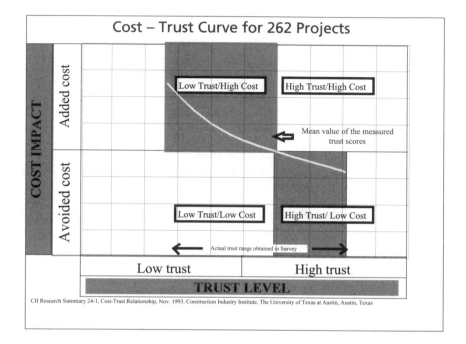

Commentary for slide 7

This research dates back to 1993, but since there is nothing more up to date that supersedes it, it is worth including. It is based on a study of 262 construction projects, involving all interested parties. Results show there is a direct correlation between trust and cost.

This is a very useful chart to show to finance directors who are concerned about the costs of change. Use it to demonstrate that direct cost savings will be made when a high trust culture is developed.

Slide 8

TD INDUSTRIES – PROFIT HISTORY

The chart that follows shows total cumulative profits over time for
TD. 1998, 1999, and 2000 continued a similar trend, but 2001–2003
have seen lower profits. I expect they will rebound again, starting next
year. I certainly hope so.

I am convinced that high trust has allowed us to be agile and
aggressive during these difficult economic times and continue to
outperform our industry. TD always emerges from difficult
times with a strengthened position in our marketplace. While we
don't have charts and graphs to demonstrate this yet, I am confident
we will have in a few years.

Jack Lowe, Junior, CEO

Commentary for slide 8

TD Industries has an interesting history which again links good people
practice to profit. This statement and the following graph demonstrate
the link between Servant Leadership and bottom line results. They
found that when the TD partners (employees) worked in an environment of trust and service, where they had responsibility for the well-
being of the company, the bottom line scored.

Slide 9

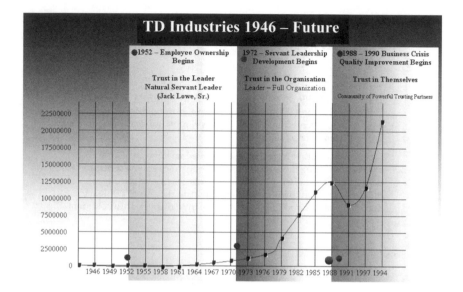

Commentary for slide 9

The dip in the chart in 1990/91 corresponds to a major downturn in the construction industry in Texas. The company weathered this because their people pulled together, giving them the edge over many competitors who went out of business.

Slide 10

HISCOX INSURANCE COMPANY

Extract from Annual Report 2002:

A strong rating environment, selective underwriting and good claims experience have contributed to a swift return to profit in 2002.

Hiscox continues to grow as a leading insurer of speciality commercial and affluent personal lines customers. By focusing on well-defined areas we can provide excellent products and services for our customers and their brokers. It is this focus and responsiveness that has allowed us to grow our aggregate gross written premium so significantly this year.

COMMENT

Hiscox were part of the syndicate that insured the World Trade Centre, so business took a major hit in 2001. Because their commitment to colleagues includes appreciating of the wisdom of experience, they were able to ride the storm and bring the business to a better position within the year.

Slide 11

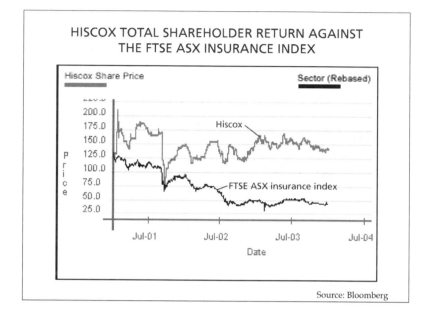

Slide 12

FLIGHT CENTRE UK Ltd

Extract from Annual Report 2002:

Having the right people in the right roles is our most important strategy and their development will be a core platform for our future direction. Emphasis will be placed on identifying and developing future leaders to help these people achieve their professional and personal goals.

Graham Turner, Corporate Managing Director.

COMMENT

That this comment comes early in the statement by the MD shows the importance placed on people throughout the business. It is no coincidence that the company has thrived despite the difficult conditions in the travel industry in 2002.

Slide 13

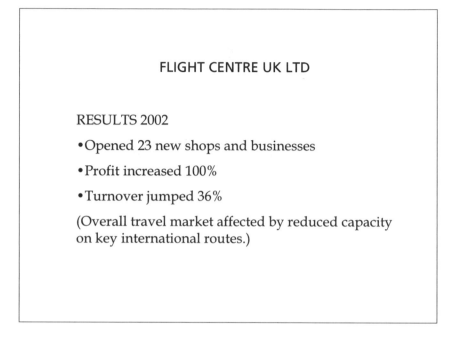

FLIGHT CENTRE UK LTD

RESULTS 2002

• Opened 23 new shops and businesses

• Profit increased 100%

• Turnover jumped 36%

(Overall travel market affected by reduced capacity on key international routes.)

Commentary for slide 13

At time of writing these results were true and growing. The fast, successful growth of this company in extremely difficult times is a testament to their culture.

Slide 14

BROMFORD HOUSING ASSOCIATION
Not-for-Profit Business Performance

- 14,000 homes in management
- £40 million turnover and estimated profit of £4m+ in 2003
- Biggest approved development programme grant allocation outside London
- Preferred partner status with 30+ local authorities
- Top 5 performer on main industry KPI's (letting, repairs, rent collection and debt control)
- Recognised national leader in provision of supported housing
- Sickness absence 2% of available working days

Slide 15

THE BUSINESS CASE FOR A GREAT CULTURE

Marianne Skelcher, HR Director, Bromford HA

•It's always cheaper to keep a customer or a colleague than lose one and have to find a replacement.

•Much of our business success is predicated on relationships. If people have good relationships with colleagues, they are more predisposed to building good and effective business relationships with partners, suppliers and other stakeholders, including customers.

•Great culture keeps morale high and absence levels low, enhancing continuity and minimising costs of cover.

•Behaviour breeds behaviour: set a positive example and others will follow suit.

Slide 16

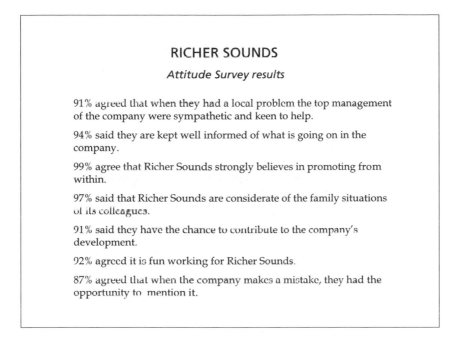

RICHER SOUNDS

Attitude Survey results

91% agreed that when they had a local problem the top management of the company were sympathetic and keen to help.

94% said they are kept well informed of what is going on in the company.

99% agree that Richer Sounds strongly believes in promoting from within.

97% said that Richer Sounds are considerate of the family situations of its colleagues.

91% said they have the chance to contribute to the company's development.

92% agreed it is fun working for Richer Sounds.

87% agreed that when the company makes a mistake, they had the opportunity to mention it.

Commentary for slide 16

These are the responses to the internal survey carried out by Richer Sounds. If you have an internal survey, find comparable questions and compare your results to the results here to show the impact of a great company culture.

If you are leading a team, use the relevant questions as a discussion point in a team meeting or team building event. How does the team compare to these high standards? Even if you are in a very different sector, these questions hold true. Make sure you leave time for a thorough discussion and look for action points at the end.

Be conscious of trust levels in the team as you ask questions. If there is low trust, don't expect to get a direct answer. Consider carefully what is said, looking more deeply than you would normally – the true answer may well be hidden. If this is difficult for you to do, ask for help from an outsider to the team or work on building trust, then ask again.

Never hold a discussion like this and not act. Don't raise expectations if you are going to ignore the outcomes.

Slide 17

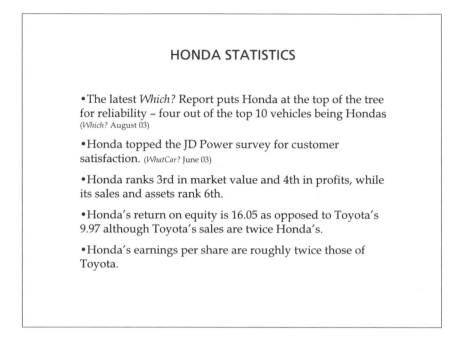

HONDA STATISTICS

- The latest *Which?* Report puts Honda at the top of the tree for reliability – four out of the top 10 vehicles being Hondas (*Which?* August 03)

- Honda topped the JD Power survey for customer satisfaction. (*WhatCar?* June 03)

- Honda ranks 3rd in market value and 4th in profits, while its sales and assets rank 6th.

- Honda's return on equity is 16.05 as opposed to Toyota's 9.97 although Toyota's sales are twice Honda's.

- Honda's earnings per share are roughly twice those of Toyota.

Commentary for slide 17

Look to the areas of excellence in your business sector. How many of them are held by your company?

If few, make a list of your competitors who hold the records and then align it to this list. The question to ask is: How much more could we do if we had a great people culture?

Slide 18

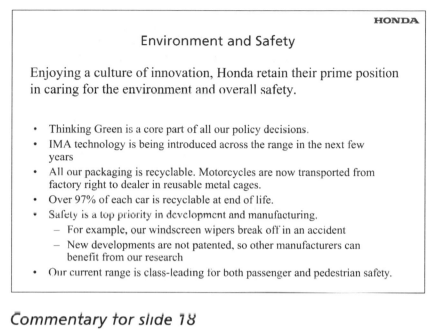

HONDA

Environment and Safety

Enjoying a culture of innovation, Honda retain their prime position in caring for the environment and overall safety.

- Thinking Green is a core part of all our policy decisions.
- IMA technology is being introduced across the range in the next few years
- All our packaging is recyclable. Motorcycles are now transported from factory right to dealer in reusable metal cages.
- Over 97% of each car is recyclable at end of life.
- Safety is a top priority in development and manufacturing.
    - For example, our windscreen wipers break off in an accident
    - New developments are not patented, so other manufacturers can benefit from our research
- Our current range is class-leading for both passenger and pedestrian safety.

Commentary for slide 18

Innovation is something that slips very easily in the pressurised world of work. In great companies, people are interested and excited about work, so they look for how to make things better.

Consider how innovative your workplace is. Would the company benefit from colleagues who are looking for the next idea and interested in taking the business forward? Use the Honda information to show how their attitude to people leads them to constant innovation, so they remain ahead of the field.

- Use them in discussion with direct reports. Ask for honest feedback and talk through how you can improve the responses for more effective team working.

The information gathered is useful as straw pole, indicating how people feel about the present culture. It can be used to stimulate a discussion about next steps.

To find out about using the full survey to gain a strong, statistically sound assessment of your company culture, look in the Useful Information section at the back of the book.

Slide 19

SAMPLE TEST STATEMENTS FROM THE
100 BEST COMPANIES TO WORK FOR SURVEY

Produced by Best Companies Ltd

• I believe I can make a positive contribution to the success of the company.

• The head of the company has positive energy.

• My manager is open and honest.

• Colleagues here care for each other.

How would your people respond?

Commentary for slide 19

This is a sample of questions from the Best Companies™ Employee Survey which forms the basis of the *Sunday Times 100 Best Companies to Work For* list. You can use them to:

- See how a random sample of people respond. NB: make sure there is no way of identifying those who have answered.

- Put the questions to your senior leaders and ask them how many people they think would answer the questions positively.

- Use it as a talking point with your peers or change champions to see what you all think would be the most likely response from the people you know.

- Use them in discussion with direct reports. Ask for honest feedback and talk through how you can improve the responses for more effective team working.

To use the full survey in your company see the Useful Information section at the back of the book.

Slide 20

INCREASE IN RECRUITMENT FIGURES SINCE BEING NAMED A GREAT COMPANY

An indication of the importance of great company culture and its ability to attract high-calibre people

Flight Centre – 200% increase in job applications since being included on the *Sunday Times* list.

Betty's and Taylor's – seldom have an application, particularly from graduates, in which the *100 Best* list is not mentioned. Since being named on the list they enjoy a better response generally from job applicants.

Hiscox – 99% of new applicants mention the fact that the company is on the *Sunday Times 100 Best* list, showing the importance of a positive workplace.

Bromford – short-listed applicants regularly mention the *Sunday Times* listing, showing that it is a factor in their choice of company.

Commentary for slide 20

When new applicants mention the list with such regularity, it demonstrates that they are keen to work in a positive people culture. Graduates want to make the most of their hard work, so seek out companies that will help further their career. The best companies are known for doing this, so will be targeted by ambitious and committed people.

Improving your work culture and becoming known as an employer of choice will increase job applications, allowing you to choose the highest calibre people. This will have a direct impact on the bottom line.

Slide 21

TIMPSON SHOE REPAIRERS

FINANCIAL IMPLICATIONS OF BEING NAMED A GREAT COMPANY

In 2001, prior to the publication of the *50 Best Companies to Work For* list, Timpson had 80% employment.

After the publication, this increased to 100% employment.

In 2002, when named as one of the *100 Best Companies to Work For*, they had a waiting list and were attracting women and graduates for the first time.

Impact on the Timpson bottom line:

In 2001 company profit = £3 million

In 2003 company profit = £6.5 million

With 80% employment you are not in a position to deal effectively with under-performance. 100% employment, plus a waiting list, means you can choose the high performers who will have a direct impact on the business.

Commentary for slide 21

This slide speaks for itself. Being able to choose the right people to work in your company has a big impact on the bottom line.

Being known as a great company has enabled Timpson to double their profit in three years.

Slide 22

CLARIDGES HOTEL

Claridges needed a major change process, so they:

- consulted the staff on what should change

- created a new mission statement

- brought managers together for an off-site meeting

- instituted daily staff briefings

- developed an open-door policy with highly visible and approachable leaders

- improved staff facilities to match front-of-house

- invited employees to stay at Claridges after three months service.

Commentary for slide 22

Claridges have made the shift from a 'dusty old British institution' to a dynamic, exciting concern. They did this by including their staff in the workings of the business.

How well do you include your people in the workings of the team? many of the actions above can be practiced, even if you are not a senior leader in the organisation. Present the story of Claridges to your team, including the results in the next slide, and see if they are interested in working with you in developing the team culture.

In a presentation to senior management, use this as an example of turning round a long established, entrenched business. A common response to a call for great company culture is that 'we are different, we have special needs, our business is so long established, we can't change now.' There can be few more entrenched organisations than Claridges which has 100 years and a lot of tradition behind it, yet they have achieved amazing results.

Slide 23

CLARIDGES – OUTCOMES 2003

Staff turnover: 1998 – 73%

2002 – 30%

2003 – 16%

• Complaints have fallen dramatically.

• Occupancy has improved by 9,000 rooms per year.

• 99% of staff are proud to work for Claridges.

All through respecting and involving staff.

Index